LINKING
DATA

NIGEL G. FIELDING
JANE L. FIELDING
both at University of Surrey,
England

Qualitative Research Methods,
Volume 4

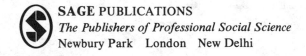
SAGE PUBLICATIONS
The Publishers of Professional Social Science
Newbury Park   London   New Delhi

For information address:

SAGE Publications, Inc.
2111 West Hillcrest Drive
Newbury Park, California 91320

SAGE Publications Ltd.
28 Banner Street
London EC1Y 8QE
England

SAGE Publications India Pvt. Ltd.
M-32 Market
Greater Kailash I
New Delhi 110 048 India

International Standard Book Number 0-8039-2563-8
0-8039-2518-2 (pbk.)

Library of Congress Catalog Card No. 85-062290

THIRD PRINTING, 1989

When citing a University paper, please use the proper form. Remember to cite the correct
Sage University Paper series title and include the paper number. One of the following
formats can be adapted (depending on the style manual used):

(1) AGAR, MICHAEL H. (1985) "Speaking of Ethnography." Sage University Paper
series on Qualitative Research Methods, Volume 2. Beverly Hills, CA: Sage.

OR

(2) Agar, Michael H. 1985. *Speaking of ethnography.* Sage University Paper series on
Qualitative Research Methods (Vol. 2). Beverly Hills, CA: Sage.

CONTENTS

ACKNOWLEDGMENTS

We are grateful to the following for permission to quote copyrighted material: C. Lacey and Routledge & Kegan Paul Ltd. for a table from "Problems of Sociological Fieldwork" in M. Shipman, ed., *The Organisation and Impact of Social Research; American Journal of Sociology,* M. Zelditch, Jr., and The University of Chicago, © M. Zelditch, Jr.

SERIES INTRODUCTION

Contrast and irony provide the definitional context for this series of monographs on qualitative methods. Contrast is inevitable, because the label itself makes sense only when set against something it is not. Irony is also inevitable, as the denotative contrast between the qualitative and quantitative is so often misleading, if not downright false. The mandate for the series is then paradoxical. We wish to highlight the distinctions between methods thought to be qualitative and quantitative, but also to demonstrate that such distinctions typically break down when subjected to scrutiny. Alongside the Sage Series on Quantitative Applications in the Social Sciences comes the Sage Series on Qualitative Research Methods, but the wise reader had best intermingle the monographs of the two sets rather than stack them on separate shelves.

One way of approaching the paradox is to think of qualitative methods as procedures for counting to one. Deciding what is to count as a unit of analysis is fundamentally an interpretative issue requiring judgment and choice. It is, however, a choice that cuts to the core of qualitative methods — where meanings rather than frequencies assume paramount significance. Qualitative work is blatantly interpretative; but, as the work in this series demonstrates, there are a number of increasingly sophisticated procedures to guide the interpretative acts of social researchers.

The monographs in this series go beyond the short confessionals usually found in the methodology sections of research reports. They also go beyond the rather flat, programmatic treatments afforded qualitative methods in most research textbooks. Not only are qualitative methods becoming more variegated, going well beyond the traditional look, listen, and learn dicta issued by traditional field researchers, they are also being shaped more distinctly by explicit philosophical and moral positions. This series seeks to elaborate both qualitative techniques and the intellectual grounds on which they stand.

The series is designed for the novice, eager to learn about specific modes of social inquiry, as well as for the veteran researcher, curious about the widening range of social science methods. Each contribution extends the boundaries of methodological discourse, but not at the expense of losing the uninitiated. The aim is to minimize jargon, make analytic premises visible, provide concrete examples, and limit the scope of each volume with precision and restraint. These are, to be sure, introductory monographs, but each allows for the development of a lively research theme with subtlety, detail, and illustration. To a large extent, each monograph deals with the specific ways qualitative researchers establish norms and justify their craft. We think the time is right to display the rather remarkable growth of qualitative methods in both number and reflective consideration. We are confident that readers of this series will agree.

John Van Maanen
Peter K. Manning
Marc L. Miller

EDITORS' INTRODUCTION

Most data analysis relies on imaginative reconstruction of the social situations, events, groups, and cultural worlds in which the data were originally lodged. If one wants rich and detailed understanding as well as finely honed measures, indices and concepts, means by which multiple methods are integrated in order to produce general explanations must be sought. The Fieldings intend this as the aim of their book. They contend that the integration of multiple methods, comparative analysis and general explanation is more talked about than done. Showing that interpretation is required for the analysis of any sort of data, and that readers learn best by example, they carefully explicate an approach linking qualitative and quantitative data. Beginning with the notion of triangulation, they illustrate its complexity and its use. They also present ways of integrating qualitative materials and conclude with examples of linking qualitative and quantitative analysis. Drawing on several different sources from their longitudinal, multi-method study of police recruit training, they quite convincingly show the value of their approach. The implicit position articulated here is that using multiple approaches increases the possibility that the link between social reality and social theory is better forged. It also implies that one might be able to work 'backward' from data analysis to social situations; that is the role of the reader. Perhaps this is a book about how to read social situations from a short book on social methods.

John Van Maanen
Peter K. Manning
Marc L. Miller

LINKING DATA
The Articulation of Qualitative and Quantitative Methods in Social Research

NIGEL G. FIELDING
JANE L. FIELDING
University of Surrey

1. INTRODUCTION

> We are now not only in a new position to raise the question of the relation between micro- and macro-social theory and methodology, but also to point out new directions in which to search for a resolution…. This direction will be heavily informed (but not bounded) by advances in the more microscopic approaches, for it is there that most theoretical and methodological developments have taken place…. Paradox[ically] it is through *micro*-social approaches that we will learn most about the macro-order, for it is these approaches which through their unashamed empiricism afford us a glimpse of the reality about which we speak. Certainly, we will not get a grasp of whatever is the whole of the matter by a microscopic recording of face-to-face interaction. However, it may be enough to begin with if we can — for the first time — hear the macro-order tick. (Knorr-Cetina 1981, pp. 41–42)

There are many books on how to go about social research. The authors of a new one must make a case for its utility. We believe there is an imbalance in the literature on methodology. While there are numerous textbooks on the methodology of both quantitative and qualitative research designs, they focus chiefly on data collection rather than data analysis. This is particularly true of those concerned with qualitative methods. The texts that do tackle the analysis of qualitative data concentrate on mechanical procedures rather than on the logic of interpretation. Equally, the even less extensive literature on the interrelation of data derived from quantitative and qualitative methods is seldom explicit about analytic procedures. Most of us are familiar with Denzin's assertion that, "by combining multiple observers, theories, methods

9

and data sources, sociologists can hope to overcome the intrinsic bias that comes from single-method, single-observer, single-theory studies" (1970, p. 313). While this seems to provide a warrant for eclecticism, little help has been extended to those who try it, piling up reams of data with disparate epistemological underpinnings and then wondering how they could be reconciled.

Advocates of particular methodologies have been concerned more with asserting or defending their accustomed lines of inquiry than with indicating the possible points of convergence with other approaches. Yet in recent texts we still encounter the assertion that "the ethnographer need not limit him or herself to a single theory as a framework within which to analyse the data" (Hammersley and Atkinson 1983, p. 181). It is hard to see how the suggestion that we "approach data with multiple perspectives and hypotheses in mind" amounts to much more than an injunction to be imaginative in pondering what our data are telling us. Such homilies pay too little attention to how researchers deal with discrepancies between discrete items of data derived from the same method, much less cases of inter-method discrepancy. Certainly, deviant cases can be very useful analytically, but the processes by which the researcher decides that this is the exception that refines (if not proves) the "rule," rather than the case that implies a whole new rule altogether, are seldom made explicit.

There is another theme to this book. The division between qualitative and quantitative research is entrenched in the core disciplines of social science. For example, in psychology there is a tension between experimental and clinical methods, while in sociology it is manifest in the separation of fieldwork and statistical work. In terms of the logic of inquiry in social science, it is apparent as a difference between hypothetico-deduction and analytic induction. The caricature of qualitative research is that it is "soft" whereas quantitative research is "hard"; qualitative researchers call quantitative researchers "number-crunchers," and the riposte of the latter is that the former are mere "navel-gazers." It would be absurd to deny a distinction which researchers feel with such immediacy, but it would be unwise not to face the issue posed by Zelditch in 1962: "Quantitative data are often thought of as 'hard' and qualitative as 'real and deep'; thus, if you prefer 'hard' data you are for quantification and if you prefer 'real, deep' data you are for qualitative participant observation. What to do if you prefer data that are real, deep, *and* hard is not immediately apparent" (p. 566).

While there is certainly a polarity between being "objective and rigorous" and "subjective and speculative," some researchers have indeed shown how these approaches complement each other and how they may be integrated in practice. A few notable scholars associated with each tradition have spoken of the value of the other; Campbell has pursued the value of qualitative work, and Everett Hughes, though emphasizing the importance of fieldwork to social research, remained methodologically eclectic. In his French Canada studies and the collaborative studies of work and occupations, he used a range of methods, and his essays advocate the use of field methods in concert with the large-scale survey. The essence of Hughes' stance remained the "comparative frame of reference" that he developed for studying different types of work, seeking common dimensions, hidden similarities, and variations on basic themes before concluding that a feature of a particular area of work really was unique. These matters are also explicit in anthropology, whose forms of data may be thought especially resistant to quantification.

It has been argued in anthropology that "observations are limited, always have been and will become progressively more so as research becomes more theory-directed and less a matter of description" (Naroll and Cohen 1973a, p. vi). In cultural anthropology there has been an increase of interest in theory-testing and theory-construction, and a decline in the simple presentation of ethnographic "facts" from single studies of single societies. Attention always given to observing, recording, and (sometimes) explaining a particular culture is now augmented by interest in using such data for creating or testing generalizations which apply outside any specific culture.

To produce general theory from the resolutely empirical data of anthropological ethnographers, one must look for the non-unique categories, discover or propose relationships among them, and then ask why such relationships exist.

This holds true whether we are asking why X is present among males but not females of one culture or present in some cultures and absent in others, or whether we are asking why there is more of X among males in one culture, or more of it in some cultures.... (T)he comparative perspective is there whether we are doing fieldwork in one or a few societies, or... sampling among a large number of societies. (Naroll and Cohen 1973a, p. vii)

The comparative approach entails a more formal and rigorous approach to the data.

This suggests a new orientation for qualitative researchers, because it implies recourse to procedures for warranting inferences and validating interpretations which have been refined by quantitative researchers. Its force hinges on the arguable assertion that culture and society are stochastic phenomena operating according to the laws of probability. The object of explanation is then to seek to establish relationships among those entities defined as variables and "constants." Statistical relationships may indeed represent underlying regularities which are not visible "on the surface," but those who reject "holistic" explanation take it that such patterns result from statistically measurable properties of observed phenomena and/or symbolic representations of these entities. Theorems can be derived from applications of mathematical logic that interrelate them in a "law-like" form. Conventionally, this emphasis on theory construction and stance toward methodology as a means for searching out and interrelating non-unique categories to support claims to generalization is put as a shift from the "ideographic" to the "nomothetic."

Objectives

We make two commonsense assumptions in approaching the problems raised by these observations. First, we would argue that ultimately all methods of data collection are analyzed "qualitatively," in so far as the act of analysis is an interpretation, and therefore of necessity a selective rendering, of the "sense" of the available data. Whether the data collected are quantifiable or qualitative, the issue of the warrant for their inferences must be confronted. (We also recognize the more limited point, made by Becker, that even the most hidebound ethnographer cannot help but be attuned to rudimentary quantitative matters; the hold of modern culture is such that in some way our observations are always "implicitly numerical.") Certain procedures for handling quantitative data may mask this qualitative element, but computer-aided statistical work still relies on the underlying assumptions of statistical theory.

Even more plainly, the most advanced survey procedures themselves only manipulate data that had to be gained at some point by asking people. Qualitative judgments must be employed each time one moves further away from the point of collection; the researcher has to consider if the question was "understood" the way it was intended, whether this class of responses is equivalent to that and so may be aggregated, and so on. One of us was once interviewed for nearly two hours on his television viewing habits as part of a market research study investigating the demand for satellite TV broadcasts. At the close, the interviewer said she would just confirm the biographical data: "Mr Fielding, you are in the 25–30 age group, aren't you?" When it was explained that this was flattering but a mistake, she said she would record that answer all the same and, since her supervisor checked 10 percent of her interviews, she was sure it would not be too much to ask that the fiction be maintained over the phone if he called. Quality control is a matter for any form of data-gathering.

Our second mundane assumption is that many people find it easier to learn by example than by attending to formal rules, principles, and procedures. Of course, example in illustration of a stated principle is more powerful still. Thus, our objective is to describe the process by which qualitative data may be related to other forms of qualitative data, and by which quantitative and qualitative data may be interrelated so as to bear most forcefully on substantive problems and research issues, by using empirical data. These data will be derived from our research on the sociology of work and organization, political sociology, and police studies. We will put particular emphasis on laying bare the interpretative and analytic procedures applied to the data in achieving final conceptualization and presentation of research results.

The emphasis we are putting forward is not concerned with establishing a new primacy in the division of social science labor. Indeed, our point concerns interrelation of researchers as well as of data. The case for multi-method work argues for an intimate, "back-and-forth" testing, critique, and synthesis between what anthropologists call "comparativists" and fieldworkers. The contributions of comparativists and fieldworkers in active awareness of each other's work stands the best chance of specifying powerful solutions (Naroll and Cohen 1973a, p. ix).

Social scientists have been widely criticized, not least by each other, for their apparent tendency to engage in unrestrained theorizing. This may account for the rather severe tone of tracts on "how to" theorize. For instance, Tatje pronounces that

> the starting point for theory building remains a logically deductive system of concepts, definitions and principles. It is from these theoretical building blocks that "hypotheses" are generated. Such theoretical propositions are usually not in themselves testable however. Usually they must first be operationalized (Tatje 1973, p. 689).

One may feel that this is all very well but hardly specific enough: we need clarification of the procedure for linking operational and theoretical definitions. Operational definitions, according to Blalock (1960), can be seen as alternative definitions for theoretical concepts, as wholly different kinds of concepts, or as indices that approximately measure an underlying variable.

The important point is that it is these which we "test," and seldom directly the propositions stated in theoretical terms. To be explicit about inferences linking test data and theoretical propositions facilitates theory-building. Comparative research often involves different operational measures of the "same" concept, and it is an acknowledgment of the numerous problems of "translation" that it is conventional to treat each such measure as a separate variable. This does not defeat comparison, but can strengthen its reliability. For example, the operational definition of Naroll's "Social Complexity Index" can be dissected into a weighted average score on the variables of settlement size, number of team types, and number of craft specialties (Tatje and Naroll 1973). Different operational definitions were rendered by Carneiro (1973) and the two versions are treated as distinct concepts. But instead of meaning that they are non-comparable, it implies that concept validity can be established. The high correlations among results of the different procedures for measuring "social complexity" is evidence of the validity of each, a demonstration that they do measure the same thing. Comparability of concepts is an empirical matter. It presents one of the major problems of conceptualization in support of macro-level analysis. The most pronounced failings are where concepts have simply been used to refer to different things, or where, having universal application, they exhibit functional variation which must be grasped before generalization from a comparative base is attempted.

Rationale

Philosophers have asked what we mean by "knowing," and how we know what we know. Epistemology has assigned terms to the activities of scientists;

scientific research entails a ceaselessly repeated cycle of observation, classification, analysis, and theory. The cycle establishes the primacy of comparative work as an integrative activity, for, as Naroll and Cohen assert, "each of us may begin at any point on the spiral he likes, but the value of his work can only be fixed by examining its relevance to the other points" (1973b, p. 30).

We may recall Donald Campbell's well-known "thought experiment," which begins by assuming that there is an objective reality that can be known. It exists separately from the knower. We are also to assume that knowledge of this reality is "neither direct nor infallible but is 'edited' by the operative referent and reflected in the convergency of observations from multiple independent sources of knowing" (Brewer and Collins 1981, pp. 1–2). There is no claim of proof for the assumed reality, only that "such an assumption makes sense out of the achievements of adaptation that characterize biological evolution, individual learning and scientific knowledge alike." Although our assumption is highly plausible, one may argue against it that a convergence toward consensus on the part of the learned reflects only a common theory of reality, not objective truth.

As Brewer and Collins assert, "theories held in common *do* affect our constructions of reality, and the problem is to disentangle shared perceptions from shared reality." Campbell has been a prime mover in seeking means to do so, and has made familiar such concepts as triangulation, multiple operationalism (Campbell and Fiske 1959), and "unobtrusive measures" (Webb et al. 1966). We would suggest that qualitative research is particularly open to redirection on the basis of such procedures, on the grounds that field researchers are "methodological pragmatists."

The rationale for our approach is related to two discrete but connected developments in recent micro-sociological work. As Knorr-Cetina has noted, sociologists have increasingly shifted their overweening notion of social order from a normative version to that of a *cognitive* order. Further, they have been less inclined to work from the premise of either methodological individualism (where large-scale actions are accounted for in terms of the dispositions and beliefs of individuals) or methodological collectivism (where behavior is governed by "laws" applying to the social whole which cannot be derived from individualistic principles), but instead have adopted a "methodological situationalism" whose relevant unit is interaction in social situations. These developments challenge the traditional juxtaposition of individual and collectivity, and of action and structure, with important consequences for the articulation of data derived from disparate sources. In Knorr-Cetina's view, "both developments point in the end towards a reconstruction of macro-social theory and methodology based upon a micro-sociological foundation, or at least based upon an integration of micro-sociological results" (1981, p. 75). Even those unwilling to accept the second, weaker, proposition recognize that these developments have inspired a more formal analysis of qualitative data, more systematic attention to the logic of research design, and renewed efforts to consider how we may argue "up" from the micro-data to identify more abstract patterns.

These efforts to fill in the interstices between micro- and macro-level call on micro-sociologists to consider what kinds of matters may legitimately be quantified and how numerical data should enter their analyses. In crude terms, it was never "counting" *per se* that was challenged, but what was counted. As Becker has argued, our analyses are always "implicitly numerical"; it is a perspective that persons in modern society cannot bracket away. But some micro-sociologists have begun to consider what kind of aggregate data they need to address macro-level and policy issues. An instance is Cicourel's analysis of social mobility, in particular the effect on mobility of experience in school:

> The laborious process whereby a student's educational career is constructed, based on evaluative summaries by the teacher in writing or during face-to-face encounters with other teachers, counsellors or administrators, is the concern of the micro-researcher. The study of this process, when combined with aggregated evaluative summaries that become part of an official record for each student, constitutes a data base for the integration of micro- and macro-concepts. (Cicourel 1981, p. 75)

When added together, the subjective evaluations of school staff form an "official biography which will act on the student's ability to be socially mobile."

Comparison between instances of a phenomenon is an important procedure in taxonomy, classification, and any work involving the designation, illustration, and verification of categories. Such procedure is vital, as its quality affects analytic work erected on its premises, such as the suggestion and elaboration of schema and typologies, commonly identified as a step in concept formation and theory-building. It is important to recognize that the procedure does not require that every aspect of phenomena be assessed when comparing, but rather that all the details of the aspects which have been selected be assessed. As Popper suggests, two things which are similar are always similar in certain aspects. Similarity always presupposes the adoption of a point of view. The simple assertion of similarity reflects the perspectival character of the interpretive process. Similarity implies possible grounds for generalization; the essential mark of interpretive work is the presence of statements whose form is "where A occurs, B follows," or "where A, there B, there C," asserting a functional relationship. Kobben asks us to consider what we do in formulating such regularities: "Do we *create* order in what is *factually* chaos, or do we *describe* order in what is *apparently* chaos?" The point is that we do both; while we do in fact create order, social phenomena are such that they allow us to do so.

The drive to generalization certainly obscures some of the fascinating and important detail of social life, but its object is not only to describe order but to explain it. Ruth Benedict's famous description of the Pueblo Indians presents a unique culture with no excesses, a marked shunning of individualism, and no striving after power; it is presented but is not explained, except as an internally consistent system. But a comparative study of twenty similar societies by Thoden van Velzen and van Wetering (1960) reveals that it is one of a group whose avoidance of uncontrolled force internally permits external aggression. Comparison with other societies suggests a causal relationship: being non-stratified and matrilocal, it cannot afford internal aggression.

In our interest in the interrelation of qualitative (micro-sociological) and quantitative (macro-sociological) research findings (data and analysis), we are aware of the great attention recently paid to building macro-theory upon a micro-basis. Such arguments keep the issue of interrelation active, but our present concern is what can be achieved using existing procedures rather than setting out another new *pro forma*. Let us consider quantitative and qualitative analysis in relation to basic examples. We may begin with the question of why people vote the way they do, considering first the positivistic, quantitative approach. First, one would set the dependent variable (namely, voting patterns). Second, the dependent variable would be related to independent variables, for example, sex, age, social class. Third, one would look for associations. We might suppose that sex "causes" a given voting pattern in perfect correlation. This would be expressed as follows.

	Voting	
	Left	Right
Male	N	O
Female	O	N

We must then seek a generalization to answer the question. There can be no generalization if we take only one case, and so we must have several cases. The method is always comparative; there can be no explanation without comparison:

	Explanation
Generalization	Comparative method

However, suppose there is not a perfect correlation between sex and voting. Then another characteristic must be involved, thus preserving the "causality" between sex and voting. One can always explain the relationship by involving more and more variables to explain the variation. This is the *variable-centered* approach (Abell 1982).

In an equally oversimplified qualitative approach to voting behavior, the researcher might proceed by asking people why they voted the way they did. This seems to afford explanation without a comparative method and without generalization. To consider another example, we might characterize decision-making thus:

In situation C,   person A intended O
person A believed if X occurred, O would result
therefore A did X

The generalization is about X and O but not about A. (The statement might be one about a mundane decision: if one switches the light switch [X] then the light comes on [O].) This analytic method is found only in the study of the social world and not in the study of natural phenomena. It does not depend on generalization. However, we might consider whether the reasoning is generalizable. How generalizable is the explanation here? We might consider that

Generalization is:
     intrinsic   quantitative methods
           to explanation in
     posterior   qualitative methods

Now let us consider the convergence of these two methods. Let us take the case of social class. We may suppose there is a correlation (X, Y) where X is socio-economic status of the parent and Y is socio-economic status of the child. This could be expressed thus:

SES p $>$ A $>$ B $>$ C $>$ SES c.

Here A, B, and C are intervening variables introduced by the quantitative sociologist to explain the relationship. But the qualitative sociologist would deduce axioms to explain the linkages (the "$>$"s).

To bring the two together, we could take the variable-centered regularities but would regard them not as an "explanation" but as "social facts" for explanation. In terms of research procedure, we might look at the survey results and then conduct interviews, or we might conduct interviews and then carry out a survey. There is nothing remarkable about this, but the results are frequently not analyzed in this way. Instead, reports often use qualitative data merely to "illustrate" the on-the-surface "hard" data of the survey.

A delineation of the contrasting perspectives will be useful when we want to consider their points of interrelation and interdependence as in Table 1.

TABLE 1   The Inter-relation of Data

Preferred Data	*Qualitative*	*Quantitative*
Most common analytic technique	Analytic induction (e.g. grounded theory)	Hypothetico-deduction
Logic of generalization	Generalization by examining (many cases of) data to determine axiom that fits all cases	Generalization by winnowing hypotheses in testing against data to see how many cases it explains

Our interest is in the mixed applications in which data from both perspectives are used together, and in the cases where analytic induction is used on quantitative data and hypothetico-deductive approach is used on qualitative data.

2. COMPARATIVE METHODS IN SOCIAL SCIENCE

The central tenets of positivism express a conception of scientific method modelled on the natural sciences. Method here is concerned with testing theories. The availability of scientific theory to test by confirmation or falsification is its primary feature. In Popper's argument, both lay and scientific reasoning are prompted by our expectations not being met, rather than by pure observation. "In confronting the problem, the cognizer makes unrestrained conjectures about possible solutions, much as nature makes chance attempts at solving particular survival problems. These conjectures are then tested against empirical evidence and rational criticism" (Richards 1981, p. 53). Science advances by replacing "unfit" theories with those that solve more problems, containing more empirical statements that have been confirmed than those they replace.

Testing involves comparing the prediction based on theory with what actually happens; theory is compared with "the facts." Great effort is made to eliminate the effects of the observer on the data by using an explicit, standardized procedure suitable for replication by others as a test of reliability. In a survey, the interviewer's behavior is tightly specified, the exact wording and sequence of questions is rigid, and probes and prompts are discouraged. If each occasion of data collection is experientially the same, the subjects will respond to the same "stimuli" and the data will be comparable. Against unstructured interviews and qualitative observation, it is charged that, since no one knows what the responses are to, it is impossible to interpret them. With no basis for testing hypotheses, it is impossible to do other than merely speculate about causal relationships.

Quantitative research is usually informed by this positivist stance and in opposition to the "naturalism" of qualitative research. Here rigid controls of the "artificial" experimental setting are rejected in favor of inspecting "natural" settings, and such investigation is done in a different attitude, one of "appreciation" rather than neutrality and social distance. Such an approach is more open to eclecticism. "A first requirement of social research... is fidelity to the phenomena under study, not to any particular set of methodological principles, however strongly supported by philosophical arguments" (Hammersley and Atkinson 1983, p. 7). Social phenomena are seen as unlike natural phenomena, it being argued that the social world cannot be understood in terms of causal relationships or "by the subsumption of social events under universal laws... because human actions are based upon, or infused by, social meanings: intentions, motives, attitudes and beliefs."

The particular characterization of positivist logic that the naturalists have criticized is the "stimulus-response" model of causal explanation; because people *interpret* stimuli, their actions are continually emergent, and simply using standardized methods cannot guarantee the "commensurability" of the data. Rather, interpretations of the same questions in an interview, for example, will vary among respondents and different occasions of asking.

Naturalism's solution is to study social settings in such a way as to gain access to the meanings that guide behavior, using the capacities we already possess as persons in society.

For example, participant observers assert that they can interpret the world in the same way as the people they study. "In the process of learning how to participate in social situations in the new society, the stranger gradually acquires an inside knowledge of it, which supplants his or her previous 'external' knowledge." Schutz argues that, "by virtue of being forced to come to understand the culture of the host society in this way, the stranger acquires a certain objectivity not available to culture members" (Hammersley and Atkinson, 1983, p. 8). Learning a new culture promotes "objectivity"; the researcher must treat it as "anthropologically strange," and thus render the culture as an object for study, by making those assumptions explicit which members normally take for granted.

The marginality of the researcher encourages such insight and enables the culture to be treated independent of the researcher's involvement. Nevertheless, such work is often confined to description: "the search for universal laws is rejected in favor of detailed descriptions of the concrete experience of life within a particular culture and of the social rules or patterns that constitute it. Attempts to go beyond this, to explain particular cultural forms, are discouraged" (Hammersley and Atkinson 1983, p. 8). The naturalist's reserve here is due to reluctance to "oversimplify" the complex social world. Thus, along with causal explanation, this stance rejects the generalizability of behavior found in experimental situations and insists on the importance of "meaning" as it is embedded in people's experience.

Thus, we may not assume that to generalize is the unambiguous hallmark of science. The dispute reflects Kant's distinction between scholars following the principle of "specification" and those following that of "homogeneity":

> This distinction shows itself in the different manner of thought among students of nature, some... being almost averse to heterogeneousness, and always intent on the unity of genera; while others are constantly striving to divide nature into so much variety that one might lose almost all hope of being able to distribute its phenomena according to general principles. (Kant 1955, pp. 5–6)

The dispute merely reflects different interests, and Kant argues that, because it does not express a fundamental ontological difference, the positions are not actually in conflict.

Nevertheless, where the assertion has been made of an ontological difference between the phenomena themselves, there certainly is conflict, an instance being Windelband's (1904) distinction between "ideographic" and "nomothetical" sciences. Anthropology seems to have been a battleground for this conflict to a greater extent than most disciplines, and the revived importance of qualitative research techniques in sociology, criminology, and social and environmental psychology has brought the debate back to the fore. Rather than fight it out in the philosophical theater, our preference is to look again at the practical procedures that researchers use. Much is to be gained by recognizing that, for example, the first hunch (inference) about the interrelationship of certain social phenomena usually comes from considering the data on one instance or one society, with a background of knowledge of other instances or societies. Inspired by his or her own data, the researcher then addresses multiple instances. We would rather deal with what researchers currently do than with the glorious but generally non-empirical accounts of the philosophers.

With the generally willing encouragement of those of like persuasion, social scientists following conventional tenets can convince others of the relevance of one level of analysis to the exclusion of the other. For example, in the study of educational attainment, quantitative analysis provides us with a notion of educational career and an indication of the level of educational goals being reached but is silent on such things as the facilitators and constraints of decisions about which courses to take experienced by students, or the processes that produce the aggregated outcomes. It takes more effort to be convincing about the relevance of both levels of analysis. But grave analytic errors can be avoided by comparative work which could not be avoided by sophisticated mathematical formulations and complex models. Andreski cites the case of the Phillips curve, showing an inverse relationship between unemployment and inflation such that one could be "traded off" against the other in calculable proportions. The curve fitted the European and North American post-1945 data and it came to have axiomatic status. Economists were appalled when it failed after 1970. Their surprise would have been less had they observed the economic history of Latin America, where mass unemployment went along with inflation throughout the period in question. Andreski comments: "no amount of sophistication in model building can compensate for the error of leaving out even one essential variable" (1983, p. 7).

One warrant for the use of comparative methods is the blunt assertion that there cannot be a micro-sociology that studies social interaction as a local, self-contained production, any more than macro-theorists can claim that macro-social structures can ignore micro-processes. Cicourel makes this point, although the pedigree of social research hardly bears him out. His position is that micro- and macro-structures "interact with each other at all times despite the convenience and sometimes the dubious luxury of only examining one or the other level of analysis" (1981, p. 54).

The challenge is to recognize that either micro-sociological or macro-sociological work bears within it indirect reference to the existence of the other, so that, in maintaining one level of analysis, one also demonstrates that the other is an integral aspect of the phenomenon. The "restrictive practices" of normal science tend to impede this:

> (E)ven researchers who focus on broader aspects of social interaction using a more ethnographically oriented approach will also create boundaries that enable them to avoid having to integrate their interview materials and field notes with survey and demographic data on the same topics. (Cicourel 1981, p. 56)

Just so, researchers who generalize from a sample survey to a larger population ignore the possible disparity between the discourse of actors about some topical issue and the way they respond to questions in a formal context. Survey researchers employ questions about hypothetical cases and elicit opinions about specific topics. Those they neglect are not part of the analysis. It is not as simple as a problem of using quantitative methods, but of the things regarded as appropriate to quantify. In working with individual respondents, "the decisions that produce actual cases and the collective discussions in which opinions and attitudes are expressed do not become the focus" (Cicourel 1981, p. 57). Interaction across levels falls victim to the division of labor in normal social science.

We may take the case of qualitative and quantitative approaches to the study of communicative competence. For the former, competence is marked by ability to use language and adhere to behavior assumed to be "normal" for the context. Observation, interview, and tape recordings will be drawn on. Quantitative research in the field works from the reference of competence to knowledge of values, norms, and customary practice, testing these by examining response to survey and interview items, including secondary analysis of government or poll data. Language use is seldom studied. As Cicourel complains, the researchers neatly manage to avoid each other's concerns. Yet this contrasts with the sense of the world that lay actors have; they have created their own "theories" and methods for achieving an integration of micro- and macro-levels of analysis. Organizations also handle complex problems of evaluation, report, and summary, and do so in spite of limited information-processing capacity. Members develop skills to summarize what happened in a meeting, a working day or week, a consultation, a criminal case. These reflect "macro-inferences" about the attainment of organizational goals or evaluate the functioning of persons, groups, and organizations (Cicourel 1981, p. 67).

Are there forms of study where comparison is unnecessary? In the anthropological distinction between *etic* analysis (using an imposed frame of reference) and *emic* analysis (working within the conceptual framework of those studied), those who do the latter argue that comparison is inappropriate. Their test of validity is the judgement of informants, not comparisons against the alternatives put by the ethnographer. But there is still comparison: it is implied in the selection of what to report and the use of terms from one's repertoire to report findings.

If, for example, I write that some of the dead of culture 2 are defined as alive, I am reflecting the fact that the issue can be delineated in my own language and the likelihood that the issue is noteworthy because studies of other cultures have dealt with the same issue or because the issue is somehow significant in my own culture. Both the usefulness of a nonindigenous language and the relevance of the topic to another culture give an emic analysis a comparative element. (Rosenblatt 1981, pp. 202–203)

We would not wish to see social science turn away from the project of causal explanation. Qualitative research has often dodged the issue and been less than willing to admit that causal modeling is one of its legitimate concerns. There is a prejudice against positivism as well as a sensible caution in light of the great difficulty of assessing the validity of claims to causal relationship. The comparative method is the only general method for testing causal relations, but there are different approaches.

The scope and the strength of relationships suggested by theory can be tested by assessing the patterning of social events under different circumstances. The experiment is the most powerful means of testing the validity of claimed causal relations. A particular factor is introduced into one situation but not into another that is identical in all respects considered relevant. By holding constant factors relevant to plausible rival explanations, and manipulating the explanatory factor, the existence of the presumed causal relation can be checked. This is subject to whether all the relevant variables have been controlled, and to the problem of "ecological validity."

The procedural model for the qualitative study that tackles the testing of theory is "analytic induction." Denzin's outline of the procedure is shown in Table 2. As Robinson (1969) has shown, analytic induction was too sharply distinguished from statistical method by Znaniecki, and its capacity to produce universal statements is derived from its concerning itself only with necessary conditions, ignoring the question of sufficient conditions. Bloor's (1978) study of recommendations of adeno-tonsillectomy by ear, nose, and throat specialists is an instance of a study which uses the method but does encompass sufficient as well as necessary conditions. The example of Cressey's study of trust violators (considered below) offers another refinement of analytic induction, to put analytic weight on exceptions. The idea is Popperian; we should search actively for exceptions because, while no finite number of confirming cases can guarantee validity, we can increase the chances of its being accepted as well-founded if we study those cases where, because of the strength of rival explanatory factors, it seems least likely to be proved correct. The important difference between analytic induction and the hypothetico-deductive method is the former's emphasis that testing theoretical ideas is not the end of scientific inquiry but a step leading to refinement of theory.

Comparative work using qualitative data is by no means ruled out. Ethnographic data can be used to test theory, for example, where cases which are crucial to a theory — those where it may be thought most likely to fail — can be examined ethnographically. The disadvantage of not being able physically to manipulate the "variables" does not rule out its use: the reduced risk of "ecological invalidity" should partly compensate for inability to control variables. As Hammersley and Atkinson (1983) argue, there is the additional advantage of ethnography's use of multiple data sources:

> This avoids the risks that stem from reliance on a single kind of data: the possibility that one's findings are method-dependent. The multi-stranded character of ethnography provides the basis for triangulation in which data of different kinds can be systematically compared.... This is the most effective manner in which reactivity and other threats to validity can be handled. (Hammersley and Atkinson 1983, p. 24)

It is to triangulation that we now turn.

TABLE 2 Methods of Obtaining Information

Information types	Enumerations and samples	Participant observation	Interviewing informants
Frequency distributions	Prototype and best form	Usually inadequate and inefficient	Often but not always inadequate; if adequate, it is efficient
Incidents, histories	Not adequate by itself; not efficient	Prototype and best form	Adequate with precautions and efficient
Institutionalized norms and statuses	Adequate but inefficient	Adequate but inefficient except for unverbalized norms	Most efficient and hence best form

SOURCE: Zelditch (1962, p. 576)

Triangulation

Our truth is the intersection of independent lies. (Levins 1966, p. 423)

The term "triangulation" derives from surveying. Knowing a single landmark only locates one somewhere along a line in a direction from the landmark, whereas with two landmarks one can take bearings on both and locate oneself at their intersection. Campbell and Fiske (1959) use triangulation to refer to situations when "a hypothesis can survive the confrontation of a series of complementary methods of testing." The usual emphasis is on combining methods, but there are also many instances of using a number of data sources (self, informants, others in the setting) or a number of accounts of events (the same person regarding an event from several "angles" for different audiences). According to a recent ethnographic text,

> Data-source triangulation involves the comparison of data relating to the same phenomenon but deriving from different phases of the fieldwork, different points in the temporal cycles occurring in the setting, or... the accounts of different participants (including the ethnographer's) involved in the setting. (Hammersley and Atkinson 1983, p. 198)

In research, if diverse kinds of data support the same conclusion, confidence in it is increased. Implicitly, this is only to the degree that different kinds of data incorporate different types of error.

Additionally, there is triangulation between different researchers, and also technique triangulation, comparing data from different techniques.

> To the extent that these techniques involve different kinds of validity threat, they provide a basis for triangulation. Ethnography often involves a combination of techniques, and thus it may be possible to check construct validity by examining data relating to the same construct from participant observation, interviewing and documents. (Hammersley and Atkinson 1983, p. 199)

The basic procedure is to check links between concepts and indicators by using other indicators. This does not complete the test. Even if results match, there is no guarantee of valid inference. There may be systematic or even random error which leads each indicator to the wrong conclusion. "What is involved in triangulation is not the combination of different kinds of data per se, but rather an attempt to relate different sorts of data in such a way as to counteract various possible threats to the validity of our analysis" (Hammersley and Atkinson 1983, p. 199).

The very flexibility of field research attracts the charge that such work is impressionistic, biased, "subjective." Although many respond by drawing on several methods in order to reduce the influence of data from any one method, set of data, or researcher, this only excites in critics the charge that the analysis has selectively drawn on multiple sources conducive to the chosen argument. Triangulation, or the multiple-strategy approach, is no guarantee of internal and external validity. However, while we may not feel that it meets the most entrenched critics, the real target for such efforts at quality control is the researcher.

When pressed about validity and reliability, qualitative researchers ultimately resort to their own estimation of the strength of the cited data or interpretation; we have heard such responses many times. Triangulation puts the researcher in a frame of mind to regard his or her own material critically, to test it, to identify its weaknesses, to identify where to test further doing something different. The role of triangulation is to increase the researcher's confidence so that findings may be better imparted to the audience and to lessen recourse to the assertion of privileged insight.

Denzin has systematized potential triangulations into four types. First, there is *data triangulation*, which may include (1) time triangulation, exploring temporal influences by longitudinal and cross-sectional designs; (2) space triangulation, taking the form of comparative research; and (3) person triangulation, variously at the individual level, the interactive level among groups, and the collective level. Second, there is *investigator triangulation*, where more than one person examines the same situation. Third, there is *theory triangulation*, examining a situation from the standpoint of competing theories. Finally, there is *methodological triangulation*, where there are two variants: "within-method" approaches, when the same method is used on different occasions (without which one could hardly refer to "method" at all), and "between-method" approaches, when different methods are applied to the same subject in explicit relation to each other.

In "within-method" triangulation, the researcher takes one method and uses multiple strategies with a view to reliability. It is a check on data quality and an attempt to confirm validity. For example, in his study of probation officers, Nigel Fielding routinely kept a set of notes as the interview progressed and at the time of transcription, both of which were additional to the data from the transcript of the taped interview. However, as Webb et al. (1966) point out, every means of data-gathering is subject to specific validity threats, and the best response is to seek a convergence of data from different classes as well as of different data from the single class; that is, we should use different methods to look at the same situation. In our study of police recruits in training, the qualitative data included the "interview aid form" completed by the recruiting officer, the essay on "why I want to join the police" by the recruit, in-depth interviews with selected recruits, with police instructors in the training school, with "tutor constables" (field training officers), with senior officers responsible for training, with local lawyers, and with politicians, plus observation of the sample recruits in the training school and on the beat. Matters identified in the interviews could be checked against performance. Such procedures stimulate an awareness that there is no one "truth," even in relation to quite specific, discrete, and limited incidents.

Turning to multiple sets of data raises questions of sampling by time, person, and situation. Different methods of investigation give rise to different sets of data, that is, different accounts of the same situation. This permits one to examine the relation of accounts to what people actually do, and to generate further accounts in relation to data already gathered. If we take the case of routine interaction in a shop, ideally one might observe behavior, making a video recording of it; next, one would gather first the customers' accounts, and then the cashier/serving person's accounts in relation to the transcript of the customers' accounts. The materials then exist in juxtaposition. The critical point is how to integrate these sources of data. Comparison of the different accounts is possible, but integration with a single narrative not only is difficult but also obscures the very complexity one worked hard to document.

Clearly, these approaches lead to complex research designs. They can be facilitated by using multiple investigators, although there is already a literature on the problems of ensuring amiable group dynamics as well as a common language for discussion of interpretation (Burgess 1984). Perhaps more fruitful, and less practiced, is the serious treatment of several theoretical positions in relation to the data. If internal and external validity is rigorously addressed, as Westie has argued, the systematic application of several theories to the research problem would be a routine part of research design. In Westie's (1957) formulation one would, first, bring together all relevant propositions; second, construct plausible interpretations for each; third, conduct the research to see which empirical relationships actually exist; and, fourth, reject those interpretations that are not empirically supported. The fifth stage would require further empirical investigation to select the best interpretations, with a sixth stage to reassess the theories from which propositions were originally derived, and, finally, the reformulation of a theoretical system based on the theoretical work. Yet, as Baldamus (1972) has shown, it is rare for researchers to indicate how theories are generated and reformulated in the course of their studies — or, indeed, how they came to be adopted. Such choices appear to be matters of caprice or biography. Again, the problem is not merely putting various accounts alongside one another, but integrating them.

The articulation of methods is addressed in Douglas' (1976) consideration of "mixed strategies," whose chief principle is that one should begin with as little control in methods as possible and with a maximum of natural interaction. Movement should be from uncontrolled to controlled methods, from natural to less natural forms of interaction. This is much the same as the stock texts which regard observational work as a nice pilot procedure which helps us to conceptualize and thus to define a more systematic instrument. In general, these approaches and words of advice reduce to little more than a suggestion to be flexible over methods. Triangulation does not mean just taking three different points of view, although in at least one case it has been taken this literally (Elliott and Adelman 1976). It seems sensible enough to commend the use of a range of methods, data, investigators, and theories in our work, although there remains no guarantee that, as some enthusiasts suggest, this will "overcome any problems of bias" (Burgess 1984, p. 146). However, here too the tough problem is not to use several approaches alongside one another, but to achieve integration.

The first tangible step toward achieving an integration of these various approaches, rather than a simple proliferation of methods, data, investigators, and theories, is given by Zelditch (1962). It becomes crucial to consider what kinds of methods and what kinds of information are relevant, and how the appropriateness of different methods for different purposes can be settled. Using criteria of "informational adequacy" (i.e., accuracy and completeness) and "efficiency" (cost per added input of information), Zelditch suggests certain combinations of method and type of information as formal "prototypes," or irreducible procedures (see Table 2). The prototype method is used as a criterion by which to evaluate other forms. Choice of method depends on a *comparative* sense.

The idea that one uses different tools for different jobs is supremely sensible, and few would summarily dismiss Zelditch's criteria of "informational adequacy" and "efficiency." But his formulation largely maintains the bifurcation of quantitative from qualitative methods by pursuing appropriate but separate use. The implication needs to be spelled out that, if all three types of information (frequency distributions, incidents and histories, norms and statuses) are sought, then all three techniques are called for. More recently, Sieber (1979), starting from this point, has considered how the respective techniques should be modified for their special roles in a set of interlocking methods.

Briefly, qualitative work can assist quantitative work in providing a theoretical framework, validating survey data, interpreting statistical relationships and deciphering puzzling responses, selecting survey items to construct indices, and offering case study illustrations. In some cases the theoretical structure itself is a product of field experience; we describe below examples of the way survey results can be validated and statistical relationships interpreted by reference to field data. Survey data can be used to identify individuals for qualitative study and to delineate representative and unrepresentative cases. For instance, we selected probation officer subsamples for interview using the data from a survey of officer attitudes to training courses; those whose attitudes were least predictable (recent training and strong hostility to it) were chosen (Fielding 1984).

Regarding data analysis, the contribution of quantitative data includes correcting the "holistic fallacy" that all aspects of a situation are congruent, and demonstrating the generality of single observations. Field methods suffer "elite bias"; over-concentration on such respondents is a natural consequence of their articulacy, strategic placing for access, and the opportunity to share their high status. Survey data can catch this fault: in our police training research the responses of low-ranking police instructors to the survey questionnaire helped us to assess the embittered views expressed by one of the senior instructors in the interview.

Sieber argues not only for the merit of multi-method work but also that certain information can be gained only by a single technique. Simple multi-method arguments assume an interchangeability for the purposes of cross-validation which is not warranted. Those who would challenge the necessity of the project, rather than the particular advantages that Sieber foresees, must demonstrate why promoting work on common problems by people working from disparate traditions is a misconceived endeavor. It must be said that social scientists have generally preferred to maintain the coherence of their preferred methods by exclusivity, rather than testing their adequacy by placing them in relation to the preferred methods of other social scientists.

Yet using multiple measures to "triangulate" on some phenomenon has a long tradition in science; Aristotle valued being able to draw on multiple explanations of a phenomenon. Pierce argued that "philosophy ought to... trust rather to the multitude and variety of its arguments than to the conclusiveness of any one. Its reasoning should not form a chain which is no stronger than its weakest link, but a cable whose fibers may be so slender, provided they are sufficiently numerous and intimately connected" (Pierce 1936, p. 141). More recently, Campbell's emphasis on multiple determination and the epistemological, ontological, and methodological consequences of its use has been highly influential.

The logic of the approach was well summarized by Wimsatt (1981, p. 126) in the following procedures:

1. to analyze a *variety* of *independent* derivation, identification or measurement processes;
2. to look for and analyze things which are *invariant* over or *identical* in the conclusions or results of those processes;
3. to determine the *scope* of the processes across which they are invariant and the *conditions* on which their invariance depends;
4. to analyze and explain any relevant *failures of invariance*.

In social science the normal procedure involves using the agreement of different tests, scales, or indices of different traits, measured by different methods, in ordering "a set of entities as a criterion for the 'validity' (or reality) of the constructed property (or 'construct') in terms of which the ordering of entities agree."

The consequence (and a test) of the procedure is that any detection methods, including those drawn from other disciplines, can do as well in indicating the presence of the studied phenomenon. For example, McClintock's (1971) study of factors affecting the reproductive cycles of women in college dormitories found that 135 women whose cycles were initially randomly timed and of different length became synchronized after several months into 17 groups having similar cycles. Group membership reflected those who spent most time together. After synchrony, group membership could be found either from data on the individual's cycle or from a sociogram focused on frequency of interaction with other dormitory residents.

The importance of "robustness" (i.e., invariance) lies not only in what it directly measures but also in its widespread but implicit use to explain that which is not robust in terms of that which is. It is also used in contexts where there is uncertainty about the status of purported properties to argue for their "veridicality or artifactuality" in order to indicate properties with which theory may be constructed.

Convergent validity is a form of robustness, and the criterion of discriminant validity can be regarded as an attempt to guarantee that the invariance across test methods and traits is not due to their insensitivity to the variables under study. Thus, method bias, a common cause of failures of discriminant validity, is a kind of failure of the requirement for robustness that the different means of detection used are actually independent. (Wimsatt 1981, p. 147)

Campbell and Fiske (1959) argue that the adequacy of any operationalization of a hypothetical construct must be settled by its convergent validity (the agreement between different methods of measuring the same construct) and discriminant validity (differentiation of results when the same method is used to assess hypothetically different qualities of the same objects). Analysis of the interrelations among multiple, independent measures of multiple constructs affords both a picture of "methods variance" (the extent that results from similar methods converge when they are supposed to be assessing different constructs) and of "trait variance" (the extent to which results from different measures of the same construct converge in their ordering of a set of objects). Size of trait variance relative to method variance indicates validity of the theoretical construct.

In an equally well-known paper, Campbell and Stanley (1963) put forward a rationale for "experimentation" in social settings in terms of the logic and validity of causal inference. Good experimental design is marked by "internal validity," the extent to which variations in the outcome variable can indeed be attributed to "experimentally controlled" variation in the treatment variable rather than other sources. If "plausible rival hypotheses" could account for observed effects, internal validity is threatened. The mark of a "true experiment" is random assignment, and this is put as the yardstick for alternative methods. Without randomization, the "quasi-experimental" design is to be evaluated by the extent to which features of the design can rule out threats to internal validity.

The essence of the triangulation rationale is the fallibility of any single measure as a representation of social phenomena and psychological constructs.

Measurements involve processes which must be specified in terms of many theoretical parameters. For any specific measurement process, we know on theoretical grounds that it is a joint function of many scientific laws. Thus, we know on scientific grounds that the measurements resulting cannot purely reflect a single parameter of our scientific theory... for a tally mark on a census-taker's protocol indicating family income, or rent paid, or number of children, we know on theoretical grounds that it is only in part a function of the state of the referents of the question. It is also a function of the social interaction of the interview, of the interviewer's appearance, of the respondent's fear of similar strangers... and so on. A manifest anxiety questionnaire response may be in part a function of anxiety, but it is also a function of vocabulary comprehension, of individual and social class differences in the use of euphoric and dysphoric adjectives [and] of idiosyncratic definitions of the key terms. (Campbell 1969)

It is not hard to pile up such doubts. In their argument for "unobtrusive measures," Webb et al. (1966) address the fact that any theory has so many elements which are not susceptible to test that points of coincidence between theoretical predictions and available measures, or "outcroppings," are, singly, bound to be equivocal. Consequently any available "outcropping" should be tested, and the more remote or independent the checks, the more "confirmatory" their agreement.

Triangulation is a procedure which is also available in the analysis of text or dialogue. For example, in anthropology, multiple iteration can take the form of "back-translation," where a bilingual person translates a text from source to target language and another bilingual person independently translates it back to the source language. The researcher may then compare the original text with the twice-translated one in the researcher's native language.

> In exploring discrepancies with the translators, the investigator discovers what contexts are considered relevant to the topic in each language, how competent the translators are in considering and selecting among appropriate alternative phrases, and which other biases each translator alone might not have been willing or able to reveal. (Levine 1981, p. 178)

When no discrepancies between the original and the twice-translated text are found, this constitutes a form of triangulation, which is simply convergent evidence that an "unbiased" translation has occurred and that the translators are competent.

The point, as Werner and Campbell (1973) have argued, is that as the original text is decoded it is promptly encoded in another language with a capacity to bias original meanings in its own "referential framework." This generates mismatches. Campbell's solution lies in the diversity of errors, here the multiplicity of paraphrases always available for rendering meaning in a language. The procedure is that of "multiple iteration" or winnowing, which involves trial and error. This procedure applied formally identifies the errors, which are then eliminated. Multiple "back translation," with its successive approximations, is the method for identifying and eliminating mismatches.

Implicit in the case for the interrelation of data from different sources is an acceptance of a relativistic epistemology, one that justifies the value of knowledge from many sources. As Campbell's work illustrates, placing research designs within a "common epistemic framework" encourages the researcher to operate supplementary procedures as checks against threats to validity, even in the case of designs which are somewhat weak. Campbell's arguments about quasi-experimental design, unobtrusive measures, and the knowledge embodied in "traditions" all emanate from a relativistic stance toward knowledge sources.

Critique of Triangulation

As we have seen, many social scientists see a wide gulf between data gained through the formal methods of quantitative research and data such as ethnographic reports, which are not fully specifiable in advance. A less prejudiced assessment than the labeling of one approach as rigid and the other as anecdotal and impressionistic may be gained if we start from a premise that emphasizes the continuity of all data-gathering processes, whether by lay persons, natural scientists, or social scientists.

Any information-gathering device is both privileged and constrained by its own particular structure and location; the qualities that enable one kind of information to be collected close off others. Campbell put forward research design strategies for assessing the limits of data by multiplying sources of information and thereby diversifying biases in order to transcend them. Researchers have often accepted this warrant for utilizing different methods on the same problem without taking up the pursuit of that which is invariant in a systematic way. The danger is that, by seizing the endorsement of multi-method research without borrowing the bias-checking procedures too, researchers avid to try new procedures simply multiply error, or pick out the points of similarity in data from procedures which may be quite incompatible. These too are consequences of declaring a common epistemic framework among data sources.

Using several different methods can actually increase the chance of error. We should recognize that the multi-operational approach implies a good deal more than merely a piling on of instruments. Campbell's multiple operationalism, the most systematic, refined, and widely-retailed approach, requires triangulated measures — but measures whose relationship is theoretically known or given, a necessity which, as Crano (1981) complains, is "not always recognized in the mundane practice of our science." In the absence of this, one might borrow the bias-checking procedure without the proliferation of methods. In Naroll's (1973) "control factor method," spurious correlations are controlled by measures of reporting bias. A "control factor" is a characteristic of the data collection process which is thought to be related to the accuracy of the final data coding; for example, in ethnography one might consider length of the fieldworker's stay, familiarity with native language, and the degree of participation in the culture.

The important feature of triangulation is not the simple combination of different kinds of data, but the attempt to relate them so as to counteract the threats to validity identified in each. "One should not, therefore, adopt a naively 'optimistic' view that the aggregation of data from different sources will unproblematically add up to produce a more complete picture" (Hammersley and Atkinson 1983, p. 199). Indeed, the differences between types of data can be as illuminating as their points of coherence.

We have argued that it is naive to assume that the use of several different methods necessarily ensures the validity of findings. McCall and Simmons long ago pointed out the fallacy into which the characterization of qualitative data as "rich" leads the novice. The novice may neglect the fact that data are never rich in and of themselves, but are "enriched" only by their being grounded in a refined theoretical perspective. Because of its emphasis on "telling it like it is," research informed by a naturalistic perspective often finds the idea of starting with a "blank mind" rather appealing. It may be a good thing to begin with no preconceptions, if this means that we have no axe to grind, no preferred perceptual grid into which data will be forced, or for which only the conformable data will be selected. Too often, it serves as a warrant to almost blindly collect quantities of "data," the value of which is uncertain and trustingly thought to be discoverable after the fact.

Two main sources of bias are apparent in qualitative fieldwork: a tendency to select field data to fit an ideal conception (preconception) of the phenomenon, and a tendency to select field data which are conspicuous because they are exotic, at the expense of less dramatic (but possibly indicative) data. These are very human failings. They are costs of a methodology which is keen to emphasize its humanism. The rigidity of positivistic methods does help researchers to resist these faults, but such work is hardly free of these problems, either. What makes it easier to trace such faults in survey research is that the character of the data, and the necessity to state hypotheses, makes the researcher's assumptions more explicit and available for inspection.

Qualitative research can pursue these benefits by specifying the role of each element of the data in the initial research design. It may then emerge that the degree of quantification offered by "systematic" observation methods better suits the purposes of a primarily ethnographic-oriented team while offering sufficient statistical data, or that considering the alternative of a systematic observational design, such as the use of Flanders' (1970) Interaction Analysis Categories, establishes the need for a survey with a larger base. Systematic observation can have some of the advantages of the survey, as in Humphreys' (1970) work on the "tearoom trade." In his study of impersonal sex in public toilets, Humphreys filled out a set of "fact-sheet"-type variables and descriptors for each observation later augmented by conventional descriptive field notes, and declared that this strategy gave "objective validity" to the data gathered; it would be more accurate to say that a quality control mechanism was built into the data by giving them physical descriptors that could be checked. Systematic observations, like surveys, facilitate replication and comparative studies, a number of variables having been controlled.

Specified matching of the degree of structure of method to the elements of the phenomenon is obviously sensible, but it is remarkable how often decisions as to which method, with which degree of structure, should be deployed are made on ad hoc grounds, or because of the vogue for certain methods (Hammersley 1984). The proliferating number of accounts of "what *really* happened on our research project" testify to the need for rigor in establishing the linkage between the logic of the research design and the chosen methodology. The multi-method design particularly demands this, but it also provides particularly clear indications of how it is to be done. Triangulation needs to be as consistent between measures as possible, and at least to specify those points at which there are divergent assumptions. For example, qualitative research designs often take a non-probability sampling line (where there is no means of estimating the probability of units being included in the sample), while survey work often pursues probability sampling (where every member of the research population has the same calculable, non-zero, probability of being selected). The language of "representativeness" needs to be used carefully when field researchers are actually pursuing opportunistic or snowball sampling, and this needs to be kept in mind when comparison is made with survey data drawn from "genuinely" representative samples. The advantages of combining methods should not lead researchers to subordinate their awareness that the different approaches are supported by different epistemologies and logical assumptions, which require their handling by different terminologies.

Articulation is the point of argument at which rigor (or its lack) is manifest. This holds for articulation of method to research problem, of interpretation to datum, and of analysis to interpretation. Needham's discussion of "Wittgenstein's arrows" (1983, pp. 155–166) shows us that even the little exercise of seeking the changes of aspect under which a line drawing of an arrow can be viewed, and working toward the abstractions suggested by the drawing, leads us to "ultimate questions" of canons of representation. In his elegant phrase, "in this region of conjecture there are no axioms, and the only tranquillity is the transient quietude of skepticism."

It is the stance we should have to all of our abstractions. We cannot work (or do anything else in life) without summary, abstract, and generalization, but we must be prepared to subject these glosses to skeptical interpretation. Rejecting absolute versions of truth, and the feasibility of absolute objectivity, is not the same as rejecting the standard of truth or the attempt to be objective. We accept the abstraction or paradigm as invitational, suggesting intrinsically the "constant and unevadable necessity for interpretation and change of aspect" (Needham 1983, p. 32) This is the paradigm's warrant.

Mulitiple triangulation, as Denzin expounded it, is the equivalent for research methods of "correlation" in data analysis. They both represent extreme forms of eclecticism. Theoretical triangulation does not necessarily reduce bias, nor does methodological triangulation necessarily increase validity. Theories are generally the product of quite different traditions, so when they are combined one may get a fuller picture, but not a more "objective" one. Similarly, different methods have emerged as a product of different theoretical traditions, and therefore combining them can add range and depth, but not accuracy. In other words, there is a case for triangulation, but not the one Denzin makes. We should combine theories and methods carefully and purposefully with the intention of adding breadth or depth to our analysis, but not for the purpose of pursuing "objective" truth.

To specify a research design systematically is to adhere to some underlying rationale. The researcher knows what, for the point of analysis in question, is to be regarded as the dependent variable and how other variables are hypothesized to affect it. The analyst has *ground rules*, but it is these which Denzin neglects. Ground rules for the selection of theories or of methods transform eclecticism into "syntheticism." It is the fact that the approaches fit together which adds to the plausibility of the researcher's interpretation. The ground rules for the selection of multiple theories and multiple methods issue from the basic and plausible assertion that life is multifaceted and is best approached by the use of techniques that have a specialized relevance.

The most apparent countenances of society are those of structure and interpretation. Simmel saw that all social life has a contextual dimension that gives it form and an interpretative dimension that provides it with content. We would argue for the necessity of synthesizing these dimensions, hoping to gain from their combination. We need to be able to read the small print of social interaction but also to make out the entity into which the pages are combined. These dual concerns become important in resolving procedural problems at each of the stages of orientation, imagination, collection, and analysis. For instance, when selecting perspectives to bring to bear on one's research problem, one should consider how much more rounded the work would be if it used one perspective from each "side" of the structuralist/ interpretativist divide. The labeling theorist could look at perspectives that give an account locating those interactions in a wider context. Those inclined to measure norms or attitudes could explore the context in which a norm for behavior becomes an action, or in which an attitude signifies more than a predisposition. Seeking out as many spurs to the imagination as possible is obviously a good idea, but, at the very least, one should try systematically to employ one method of prompting thought on structure and one on actual interaction.

It is impractical and unwise to list all the available means of data collection and analysis and use as many as possible. What is important is to choose at least one method which is specifically suited to exploring the structural aspects of the problem and at least one which can capture the essential elements of its meaning to those involved. Our study of children convicted of grave crimes initially focused on what it meant to be prosecuted for murder as a child, using in-depth interviews with children and observation in custodial centers. However, it was not necessarily the same kinds of children who were prosecuted in the recent past as those prosecuted prior to various legal changes which widened the definition of "grave crimes." To be adequate at the level of structure, the account had to be situated in a framework gathered from a larger sample over a longer period. Our quantitative analysis not only provided a descriptive overview of the phenomenon but revealed a dramatic increase in prosecutions, which in turn suggested the need for research on the attitudes of judges in such cases (Godsland and Fielding 1985). The implication is to incorporate at least one method of data collection that describes and interprets the context in which the interaction occurs and one that is designed primarily to illuminate the process of interaction itself.

Multiple theories and multiple methods are indeed worth pursuing, but not for the reasons Denzin cites or the way he suggests. The accuracy of a method comes from its systematic application, but rarely does the inaccuracy of one approach to the data complement the accuracies of another. That may be true for attempts to assess the significance of one aspect of social structure or for one element of interaction, but not for those who try to explore the interrelated features of society. The need to draw theory and methods from both elements of the dual traditions at its simplest means that researchers who are drawn to explore an organization by administering questionnaires should also stimulate their imagination on the nature of the interactions contained within the organization, asking themselves whether breadth or depth might not be added by adopting techniques to elicit the meaning of complex interactions. Similarly, researchers impressed by the subtleties of, say, the probation officer/client relationship should not throw everything at this problem but should also ask themselves whether the political economy of criminal justice does not provide an understanding of the constraints and opportunities which determine the parameters for that interaction. A dualist view, if not full-blown "triangulation," is to be recommended, in order to meet the need to describe the detail of the foreground against the design of the background.

Logic and Interpretation

To address the nature of interpretation, we have to consider the logic of argument. An argument (or analysis) consists of connected statements; a good argument is when "the connections are made by logically valid inferences and in which the substantive components are factually correct" (Needham 1983, p. 19). Durkheim charged sociologists to consider social facts as things. By this he meant a stance taken by the sociologist. "To treat facts of a certain order as things is... not to classify them in some category or other of reality; it is to observe a certain mental attitude toward them" (Needham 1983, p. 20). Their characteristic properties cannot be discovered introspectively, but by approaching them as if we know nothing at all about what they are. Our stance is detached. "It is not that social facts are objective things, but that we should consider them objectively as though they were things."

This approach to "interpretation" is guided by the particular cast given to the hermeneutic project by Hans Gadamer, especially his stance toward "tradition" as the whole of the person's cognizing apparatus as it is grounded in his or her experience up to the point where a problem stimulates reflection. The implication is that this pertains to the interpretation of both quantitative and qualitative data, although proponents of the latter have been particularly open to it. The sorts of contextual matters and holistic explanation Gadamer's argument commends have seldom been conducive to survey researchers.

> A reflection on what truth is in the human sciences... must be aware of the fact that its own understanding and interpretation is not a construction out of principles, but the development of an event which goes back a long way. Hence it will not be able to use its concepts unquestioningly, but will have to take over whatever features of the original meaning of its concepts have come down to it. (Gadamer 1975, p. xiv)

The particular conditions under which social knowledge has arrived at its present position must be recognized, and their bearing on interpretations made explicit.

The search for "regularity" in observed phenomena is integral to the conventional scientific search for universal laws of relations between objects, but Gadamer asserts that the yardstick of an increasing knowledge of regularity betrays a misunderstanding of the nature of human sciences. We should try to grasp the concrete phenomenon as an instance of a general rule.

> The individual case does not serve only to corroborate a regularity from which predictions can in turn be made. Its ideal is rather to understand the phenomenon itself in its unique and historical concreteness.... the aim is not to confirm and expand these general experiences in order to attain knowledge of a law, e.g., how men, peoples and states evolve, but to understand how this man, this people or this state is what it has become. (Gadamer 1975, p. 6)

Generality is not most usefully the assertion that one has identified a law of behavior which works this way everywhere, but the argument that within it this instance of a phenomenon contains all its precursors, including the thought toward it of its previous interpreters.

We should relate the argument to the procedures for interpretation. Although he introduced the effective notion of "point of view" from Leibniz's study of optics, Chladenius, an eighteenth-century scholar, actually saw interpretation as an occasional and pedagogical pursuit. Interpretation involved "adducing those ideas that are necessary for the perfect understanding of a passage," but did not serve to indicate the "true understanding" of it. "Understanding" and "interpretation" were different. For the most part, understanding was immediate, registering meaning on the surface. Even so, interpretation had become important, not the least reason being the critical and questioning spirit of the period. Gadamer points out the importance of Chladenius' recognition that understanding the author is different from understanding the writing.

> The norm for the understanding of a book is not the author's meaning. For, "since men cannot be aware of everything, their words, speech and writing can mean something that they themselves did not intend to say or write," and consequently, "when trying to understand their writings, one can rightly think of things that had not occurred to the writer". (Gadamer 1975, p. 162)

The point is significant. The utility of the interpretative effort is its suggestion of plausible alternatives: "unfruitful passages can become fruitful for us" as they "encourage many thoughts." The notion of interpretation carries with it the presumption that there is more than what is on the surface of the text, or datum, and that the observer's perspective can transcend the author's — or the actor's. (This, incidentally, endangers the idea of a "member test" as an index of validity in qualitative fieldwork.)

By writing of "tradition," Gadamer invokes reference to the contextual matters which enable interpretation but are no part of an "existent world." Husserl's phenomenological concept of the "life-world" is an explicit counter-formulation against the concept of the world that includes those things which can be made objective by natural science. This world is essentially related to subjectivity; it "exists in a movement of constant relativity of validity." While Husserl was not afraid of the "spectre" of relativism, others are. Husserl's stance can be as troublesome for ethnomethodologists as for survey researchers. But it has one other relevant point for us. Husserl argues that we cannot conceive of subjectivity as antithesis to objectivity; by doing so, our concept of subjectivity would be conceived in objective terms. Instead, he commends a "correlation research" which takes the *relation* as the primary thing. The "poles" into which it forms itself (as with "understanding" into "subjective" and "objective") are contained within it. Gadamer cites Husserl's criticism of

> the naivete of talk about "objectivity" which completely ignores experiencing, knowing subjectivity, subjectivity which performs real concrete achievements, the naivete of the scientist concerned with nature, with the world in general, who is blind to the fact that all the truths he acquires as objective, and the objective world itself that is the substratum in his formulation, is his own life construct that has grown within him, is, of course, no longer possible. (Gadamer 1975, p. 220)

Blind it may be, but impossible it is not. We must now consider what these arguments mean for our stance toward interpretation. The early arguments of Chladenius reflected a tension between interpretation and understanding. We may now argue, with Gadamer, that "interpretation is not an occasional additional act subsequent to understanding, but rather, understanding is always an interpretation, and hence interpretation is the explicit form of understanding" (1975, p. 274). Indeed, the very language and concepts of interpretation are themselves an "inner structural element" of understanding. What is important is that we accept the inevitability of the need to interpret, founded on an acceptance that absolute objective knowledge, in light of the concepts of "tradition" and the recurrent play of "the life-world" on our scientific projects, is a standard, but not a *practical*, goal. If we accept that all our pronouncements must be regarded as interpretations, and that neither qualitative nor quantitative data enjoy special claims to treatment as "objective," the necessity to warrant inferences closely in relation to data becomes a discipline in helpful tension with our desire to experience and express the phenomenon in holistic and general terms.

Notable early social investigators, such as Mayhew and Booth, employed both quantitative and qualitative methods, regarding them as complementary. The Chicago School, long associated with naturalism and observational methods, also used statistical methods, and generally agreed on the value of both. It was only with the rapid development of statistical methods, and the rising influence of positivist philosophy, that survey researchers came to regard their work as a self-sufficient methodological tradition, against which naturalism emerged as a reaction.

Importantly, survey researchers have acknowledged the force of several naturalistic critiques: the difficulty of inference from response in experimental conditions has given us the notion of "ecological validity," the effects of researchers and the research process on response has led to a genre of work on quality control, and the emphasis on needing to apprehend meaning from the subject's perspective has made it quite routine to carry out unstructured pilot interviews and observation prior to survey research. But, as Hammersley and Atkinson note, positivists have not given up a vital part of their position, the emphasis on causality.

> They are understandably reluctant to abandon experiments and surveys in favor of exclusive reliance on ethnography. Even less are they inclined to accept naturalism's rejection of causal explanation, and in our view they are quite correct in this. While many of them have yet to realize the full implications of what is valid in naturalism, they are certainly wise not to embrace it *in toto*. (Hammersley and Atkinson 1983, p. 11)

Artificial experimental settings are not necessarily ecologically unrepresentative, nor is it the case that working in the "natural setting" always meets the problem of "ecological validity." There are real problems of reactivity, bias, and distortion, and spatio-temporal variation in observational work. Further, the "artificial" setting is still a part of society and is subject to the processes of "symbolic interpretation and social interaction" with which naturalists are so much concerned. It implies that the work of the latter can inform quality control in the positivist tradition, as it already has.

It is one thing to acknowledge the view of social action as importantly formed around interaction in which interpretation is an issue for ordinary people as well as researchers, but it is quite another to rest purely with description, seeking only to bring the perspectives of social actors into understanding. Inductivist methodology is misconceived in this respect. Even in a very small-scale setting we could not begin to describe everything, and any description we do produce is inevitably based on inferences. As Hammersley and Atkinson show, naturalism tends toward the dubious assumption that all perspectives and cultures are "rational," so that any attempt to explain them by material interests or "ideological distortion" interferes with understanding.

> While the usual consequence of relativism — the erosion of any possibility of knowledge — is avoided, the cost is nevertheless very high: social research is limited to cultural description. Anything more would imply that the cultures under study were false, being the product of social causation rather than of

culture members actively constructing reality. (Hammersley and Atkinson 1983, p. 13)

The absurd consequence is the paradox that, while culture members themselves check claims against facts and employ causal explanations, the researcher must refrain from the same. Naturalism secures its "escape from relativism" only by artificially separating theories of how members and researchers make sense of social reality.

All social research bears certain features of participant observation — the researcher participates in the social world in some role or other and reflects on the "products" of that participation, and this is no different from what people routinely do. Rather than trying to eliminate the effects of the researcher, we should set about understanding them. Schuman (1982) has expressed this clearly:

> The simple approach to survey research takes responses literally, ignores interviewers as sources of influence, and treats sampling as unproblematic. A person who proceeds in this way is quite likely to trip and fall right on his artifact. The scientific survey, on the other hand, treats survey research as a search for meaning, and ambiguities of language and of interviewing, discrepancies between attitude and behavior, even problems of non-response, provide an important part of the data, rather than being ignored or simply regarded as obstacles to efficient research. (Shuman 1982, p. 23)

To understand the effects of the research intervention, data in which the character of reactivity varies are compared.

> The fact that behavior and attitudes are often not stable across contexts and that the researcher may play an important part in shaping the context becomes central to the analysis. Indeed, it is exploited for all it is worth. Data are not taken at face value, but treated as a field of inferences in which hypothetical patterns can be identified and their validity tested out. Different research strategies are explored and their effects compared with a view to drawing theoretical conclusions. (Hammersley and Atkinson 1983, p. 18)

While this flies against the stress on description, it is much in harmony with analytic induction procedures, including "grounded" theorizing.

Many positivists and naturalists agree that the primary goal of social research is the derivation of adequate theory. Naturalism does contribute the idea that the development and testing of theory are linked and that neither has greater priority. That is, analytic induction more aptly characterizes the actual theorizing process than does hypothetico-deduction. The research process must be acknowledged as contributing to theorizing, for an eye to the effect of our procedures on the data facilitates interpretation.

It seems that the sins of naturalism have been visited on sociology as a result of a misreading of Weber, and particularly the approach taken in the Protestant Ethic essay, where sociology seemed to claim a methodological authority among the social sciences. It is often seen as arguing that to "understand" social action is to refer overt human conduct to the motives and intentions experienced by the actors; that to discover the causes of action one needs to apprehend the motives entertained by the actor. Such an emphasis is mistaken. Rather, to understand, one constructs a coherent motivational complex which enables the action to "make sense" to the interpreter (Poggi 1983). Thus, the linkage of the complex and the action is not causal but logical. "Even if a language of motives is used, one needs to bear in mind that 'motives' are attained through logical analysis, not psychological empathy, and as such they are imputed to the actors rather than 'discovered' in their consciousness" (Bauman 1984, p. 17). Weber proposed an "elective affinity," not a causal relation, between Protestant asceticism and capitalist enterprise, the logic being the "motivational complex" expressed by Protestant beliefs made sense of economic activity which resulted in profit without sensuous pleasure.

Thus, the matter of *verstehen* has often been misrepresented. It is not about somehow placing oneself "inside" the author's subjective experience, but about understanding the text by grasping what Wittgenstein called the "form of life" that gives it meaning. "Understanding is achieved through discourse; *verstehen* is therefore detached from... Cartesian individualism... and instead related to language as the medium of intersubjectivity and as the concrete expression of 'forms of life', or what Gadamer calls 'traditions'" (Giddens 1976, p. 56). Betti's (1962) review of the premises of hermeneutics identifies four principles which underwrite our assessment of the interrelation of qualitative and quantitative data in this context: first, an object is to be understood in its own terms; second, it has to be understood in context; third, it must conform to the "actuality" of experience of the interpreter ("pre-understanding"); and fourth, interpretation must be adequate in relation to the intentions of its originator ("meaning equivalence").

These injunctions are not particular to either qualitative or quantitative methods, for the vital distinction is between physical reality and social reality per se. Schutz's review of the differences stressed the subjective element which infuses any attempt to study human behavior:

> The world of nature, as explored by the natural scientist, does not "mean" anything to the molecules, atoms and electrons therein. The observational field of the social scientist, however,... has a specific meaning and relevance structure for the human beings living, acting and thinking therein. (Schutz 1954, p. 266)

While this establishes that a concern with subjectivity (and associated issues of selectivity, hence with sampling) is intrinsic to social science, for a variety of unwholesome reasons, which Becker might characterize as "low motives," quantitative researchers have been better able to mask the necessity of holding such reservations in their work. Meanwhile, qualitative researchers have made a virtue of it by emphasizing the search for "meaning(s)."

Nevertheless, it is not only ethnographers who have been interested in "meaning" as it arises from experience of the world. Burgess states that, "although social scientists have a range of approaches for studying the social world — experimental methods, statistical measures and survey research — none of these methods can fully encapsulate the subjective elements of social life" (1984, pp. 78–79). As we argue below, such "full encapsulation" is hardly a credible goal for any researcher; even the deepest "gone-native" anthropologist faces problems of marginality. People certainly have turned to observation to get at the meanings that participants assign to social situations, but Burgess, like others, seems too hastily to assume that such interests have not also been present in survey research. Many of the standard techniques of such work derive from social psychology, a field with equally keen interest in "meaning." Attitude research has been a good deal more sophisticated than its critics often assume (Deutscher 1973) in seeking refinements of procedure which increase the realism of the situations with which questionnaire items are concerned. It is important that Schutz's critique is a blanket one which arises from the nature of the topic and not the routine ways of approaching it.

Followers of a naturalistic sociology have pursued a test of congruence or principle of verifiability. The essential argument is that in any natural setting there are norms or rules of action in which actors are competent. Understanding on the part of the observer is achieved when the observer learns the rules. The adept observer is able to provide others with instructions on how to pass in the same setting. Following such a recipe, one ideally should be able to have similar experiences, becoming a member of the setting, and hence personally to appreciate the truth of the description (J. Hughes 1976).

The criteria of subjective adequacy suggested by Severyn Bruyn (1966) are good instances of this emphasis. These stress the achievement of intimate relations with members in terms of time, place, status, language, and strategic activities. In his sixth index, "social consensus," the criterion of adequacy is fulfilled by maximizing confirmation of the group's expressive meanings, either directly — by checking interpretation with subjects — or indirectly — by observing what subjects say about an interpretation.

As to analysis, the essence of the procedure is that one works "up from the data" rather than selecting some theory by convenience or whim and dipping into the data for fragments that support it. In Becker's "sequential analysis," the researcher "steps back" from the data between observations, so as to reflect on their possible meaning. Further data-gathering is directed to matters to which the observer has become sensitive by provisional analysis and leads to a refinement of hypotheses.

Sequential analysis procedures make data analysis an integral part rather than a later stage of methodology. Three chronological stages may be identified; the illustrations are from a comparative study of two new York police precincts (Reuss-Ianni 1983). Stage 1 is the *selection and definition of events, concepts, and indices.* Here, Reuss-Ianni sought activities for observation which appeared likely to give the most understanding of the social and occupational significance of precinct organization. The search was also for indicators of how such activities are organized into the continuing life of the precinct. This stage enables the researcher simply to determine that given phenomena exist or that some are related. Stage 2 is to *check on the frequency and distribution of phenomena*. Having gathered numerous "provisional" events, concepts, and indicators, the researcher must select some for concentrated attention. This is done by "continual comparative analysis" of the data. In the police study, the fieldworker determined whether the events that prompted the development of the indicators provisionally identified were typical and widespread in the precinct and how they were distributed among categories of people and segments of the organization. Stage 3 is to *construct models* of structures and codes of rules defining the socio-cultural context, here, of precinct structure and organization. Individual findings were integrated in a generalized model of the social organization of the precinct and the codes of rules identified in Stage 2.

The evaluation of hypotheses hinges on indices of the adequacy of data such as those suggested by Bruyn, plus ongoing consideration of the fit of one's observations to theory. Our hope for getting "behind" the signs which our data comprise is to attend to the relations between interpretative sets. Our handle for analytic purchase is intersubjectivity. Negotiations over meaning (between co-participants, be they peers in some social group or the special case of researcher and researched) are occasions for grasping these actors' "meanings" at this juncture. In ethnography we are available not only to hear such references as may naturally occur, but to make use of ourselves as an analytic device by an act of imagination.

There are epistemological as well as practical problems with the principle of "verifiability" as a test of adequacy. Schutz's "principle of adequacy" for social science concepts constitutes a "member test"; concepts must be built "in such a way that a human act performed within the life-world by an individual actor in the way indicated by the typical construct would be understandable for the actor himself as well as for his fellow-men in terms of common-sense interpretation of everyday life" (Schutz 1967, p. 44). However, as Giddens shows (1976 p. 33), the "principle of adequacy" is unsatisfactory because it is not clear what is involved; if it refers to matching concepts against action, this is so obvious as to be trivial, while if it implies (as is often thought) translation into terms recognizable by lay actors, it is not specified how this could be done without anticipating in the translation just exactly the thing it is intended to test.

In natural science, replication is a vital part of the test for the generalizability of axiom. In social science there is a rhetoric of replicability, reliability, and "follow up studies" which masks the actual gross neglect of replication. If anything, this is more true of qualitative than quantitative research. There is a case for not worrying about this. As Kidder maintains regarding observation, "what matters is that each additional piece of evidence is *consistent* with the other observations and not that each observation is *identical*.... Reliability in fieldwork lies in an observation's not being contradicted and proved wrong rather than its being repeated in detail (Kidder 1981, p. 248). There is an engaging story of a disagreement between Becker and Campbell over exact replication. Cynically, Campbell argued that fieldworkers are not interested in replication; they all want to make a "unique" discovery of their own. This strain to pursue the new would hijack even the student who began with the aim of replication. Becker's rejoinder was that Campbell was right, but that it did not matter because the reliability of field study data was in its not being contradicted rather than in its being exactly repeated. This applies to reliability between studies as well as within one study. "(R)ather than test-retest reliability, or research-replication reliability, qualitative research calls for something akin to an internal consistency measure of reliability. What matters in each instance is that there be no negative or inconsistent evidence" (Kidder 1981, pp. 248–249).

We have already considered triangulation as a procedure available to qualitative researchers. Effectively, the opposing approach is "respondent validation," whether the subjects whose beliefs and behavior are described recognize the validity of such accounts. Members may indeed have knowledge extra to what is available to the researcher, notably that comprising the context of studied decisions or processes. Let us leave on one side the practical difficulties of doing such feedback. There is still no reason to assume that members have privileged status as commentators on their actions. Meanings must be reconstructed for the researcher, and the evidence for them may be forgotten. Those who lie cannot be detected by polygraphs if they believe they are telling the truth. The accounts of members must be closely checked for threats to validity. There are many reasons and interests which can lead members to misreport to the researcher, and it must be borne in mind at all times that they have different purposes from the researcher's. How one handles feedback that is critical of one's analysis is not satisfactorily explained. Whatever their reactions, such feedback cannot be taken as direct validation or refutation of the observer's inferences. Rather, such processes of so-called "validation" should be treated as yet another valuable source of data and insight. Despite these problems, this emphasis on the "member test" runs through conventional naturalist methodology. Instead of a concern with the logic of validation, a concern with the mechanical procedures of data collection is characteristic.

Yet qualitative data have features which can support comparative validation procedures. If multiple measures are to remove the effects of bias by generating a "heterogeneity of irrelevancies" in each measurement, ethnographers need a sense of when irrelevancies on one topic are low and on another are several and important. The matter cannot be resolved by a rigid principle, but the situation is not hopeless. The simple reason is that ethnographers seldom use multiple sources for what they report; data for different analytic themes are drawn from different sources but are infrequently drawn together to illuminate one theme. There are good practical excuses for this — for example, the difficulty of recruiting informants at all, let alone going "behind their backs" to check their statements. But ethnographers are also sensitive to the need to spend maximum time on careful study, and there are no practical reasons why qualitative data are unsuitable for such uses.

Qualitative data have another feature which can support a comparative validating procedure. The data are "rich," or intensive. It is plain that people find such vivid material useful in evaluating an analytic framework. It helps resolve unclear meanings of terms and principles, its concreteness makes generalizations more memorable, and this enables the review of one's memory for comparable cases and facilitates probing for internal consistency.

> If generalizations and principles are being taught, the skeptic has no basis for evaluation until there is some evidence to winnow. Even a single unconvincing or faulty illustration can provide one with a sense of the invalidity of a proposition. There is typically much more information with which to do a degrees-of-freedom analysis, more material with which to do conceptual challenging and pattern matching, in a case report than in a summary of a multivariate statistical analysis on a large sample. (Rosenblatt 1981, p. 215)

Indeed, qualitative research is not as different from quantitative work as one may imagine. When qualitative researchers pursue explanation, they implicitly rely on some tenets of experimental research design. Internal validity matters in any research concerned with causal relationships. Yet the claim to study causality is often fudged by qualitative researchers. They often demur from the claim, alleging their work is "primarily descriptive" or "suggestive" or even "invitational." These are retreats to a safe position that "cannot be attacked because the writer does not claim to know what caused what" (Kidder 1981, p. 229).

Apart from timidity, there is an important reason for this. Qualitative work is inductive rather than deductive. One does not start with a hypothesis, but rather generates hypotheses from the data. "Analytic induction" reverses the procedure of hypothetico-deduction, which works from the "top" down. Instead of beginning with theoretical premises, predicting a pattern of results, and examining the data to test the deduction, one starts with data, then develops theoretical categories, concepts, and propositions (Glaser and Strauss 1967). One may well feel inhibited from claiming causal explanation in the awareness that forming hypotheses to fit the data violates normal principles of quantitative research.

However, when qualitative research presents an account of a career or socialization process, as it often does, it necessarily makes causal assertions. The steps in a socialization path are links in an asserted causal chain. A stock instance of causal explanation from qualitative data is Becker's (1963) account of becoming a marijuana user. This was a study based on retrospective self-reports to indicate career pattern. Becker's causal assertions are simple: to use the drug for pleasure one must (1) learn the inhalation technique; (2) learn to perceive the effects; (3) learn to enjoy them.

The three-stage model can be seen as a time-series design, where X is "treatment or cause" and O is "observation or effect." As Kidder points out, the difference between Becker and the conventional time-series design is that the X's are not single causes but an amalgam of necessary conditions and the X's and O's are measured retrospectively by self-report rather than by observation (Kidder 1981, p. 232). Becker's data were from people who, having tried marijuana, continue or quit as a consequence of the presence or absence of the three conditions noted above (technique, effect-recognition, pleasure), and his evidence for the assertion that these three particular conditions must be there in any regular user in reported cases where one or more condition was not fulfilled and the person did not become a user.

In his study of parole officers, McCleary (1977, p. 576) cites five career contingencies that cause them to ignore crimes: (1) to report in full reduces free time; (2) it can lead to the need to defend decisions in formal hearings; (3) reporting bad behavior is thought to reflect on the officer's own perceived effectiveness; (4) it creates "busy work" for officers; and (5) it constrains officer discretion in giving offenders a second chance. These are definite statements asserting that one thing leads to another, and their plausibility rests on the successful elimination of alternative interpretations.

McCleary's study used field notes from observations alongside informant reports, and is an exemplar of how qualitative researchers can handle threats to internal validity. The cause statement was that "routine career contingencies reward parole officers for underreporting deviant behavior.... the exceptions to this rule are situations where the parole officer realizes some benefit from reporting an incident." Unlike Becker's model, McCleary's five causes of underreporting need not occur together or in sequence. He did not design the research as a time-series or anticipate the causes. They were derived from analytic induction, so the "design" was retrospective. Even so, the design can be apprehended and the validity of the causal model assessed.

Such was the approach taken by Kidder when she worked through Campbell and Stanley's (1966) and Cook and Campbell's (1979) list of threats to internal validity (selection, history, maturation, testing, instrumentation, regression, mortality) using McCleary's study. For example, the effect of *history* is considered. The logical possibility exists that something like a change in departmental regulations could precipitate underreporting, but McCleary monitored the officers over time, finding that each had to learn to write brief reports, and that the shortened reports did not appear simultaneously, so no single event was consequential. Regarding *maturation*, the officers' underreporting behavior might have been linked to fatigue or sophistication, but McCleary noted that, no matter how fatigued, the officers would give full reports when contingencies changed.

Kidder's assertion that no observation study has ever explicitly discussed these threats to internal validity seems rather bald, but she does make the sound point that they are even better placed to do so than outsiders with an interest in rigorous method because they have more data to draw on than what appear in print. Ultimately, observers rule out such threats, not by an explicit design but by "the richness of the data," longitudinal observations, and the "nonsimultaneity of treatments across persons" (Kidder 1981, p. 240). The information that helps assess validity is generally collected without foreknowledge of its utility, but in consequence of ethnography's ground rule to record as much as possible.

An important distinction between quantitative and qualitative researchers is over the assumption that human conduct can be described and predicted from variables which characterize social actors. It is an important support for the great bulk of survey research collecting attitude data. It is not accepted by qualitative sociologists, who generally maintain that social situations are their own form of reality, having a dynamic and organization which cannot be predicted from data about the attributes of single actors. In many such critiques the complaint is not about the destination, the discovery of patterned behavior at the macro-level, but about the route. These are the critiques which are most worth examining.

It is important to recognize that the challenge to macro-sociology arising from qualitative methodology does not rule out the preoccupations of macro-sociologists. However, it does assert that the process of data generation is bound up with the outcomes obtained, and cannot be brushed aside by statistical "cleaning operations." Many qualitative researchers feel their studies are supremely empirical; their materials are "the only empirical reality there is." In their view, using the term "hard data" to mean numerical evidence is misleading because such data are several assumptions removed from the referent of the term in the experimental sense. Collins dissects the example of a numerical social mobility measure:

> First, there is the actual empirical situation in which an interviewer confronts a subject with a question. Micro-sociologists concerned to be strictly empirical examine this situation to see just in what senses the procedures of formally asking and answering such questions create the kind of data produced. Beyond this, there is the process by which the subjects transform an enormous amount of their previous social experience into a few words: their "father's occupation" and their "own occupation" can be rendered in two words, but they summarize materials that empirically, minute by minute in their previous lives, consisted of a variety of social interactions, negotiations, efforts, cognitions. The processual detail by which their career was actually made is compressed into a few nouns, given a hard and object-like form, and thence enters into the sociologists' fund of "data". (Collins 1981, p. 84)

One might add other analytic operations intervening between empirical "reality" and measure, including the interpretative work of coders, operations in which responses are re-sequenced and juxtaposed, and the various transformations of these numbers guided by statistical theories, mathematical conventions, and sociological theories. "The final product depicting 'social mobility' in tabular form... has the appearance of thing-like reality. However, it is... the product of numerous transformations of the basic empirical materials — the long sequences of social behavior — which alone have sensory, time-and-space reality" (Collins 1981, p. 84). The capacity to doubt and to seek yet stronger proofs is a necessary part of the critical, that is, the scientific, attitude. Before we are driven back to working as we always have by the magnitude of the task, we should consider where Collins' position leads him. He argues that, in order to give a full explication which dismantled every gloss en route to our measure of mobility, we would need to explicate every cognitive moment in the lives of every individual included in the mobility rate measure, taking at least as long as the total time of all the lives involved. Yet this patent absurdity reflects the quest for an absolute ideal of truth, whereas it is quite possible, and indeed the routine practice of social actors, to live with a pragmatic ideal of truth concerned with achieving successively more refined approximations rather than some final "truth." Conceding that glosses, as in the use of samples and summaries, are inevitable, he declares: "the task of micro-sociological critique should not be to prevent us from doing it, but to enable us to do it better; indeed, to point us to the crucial junctures at which macro-institutions are reproduced or changed" (Collins 1981, p. 90).

3. LINKING QUALITATIVE DATA

In this chapter we will examine the procedure and rationale involved in the concurrent use of two forms of qualitative data. This is one of the most common forms of methodological interrelation, a frequent combination being participant observation and ethnographic interviews. It occurs in academic research but also increasingly in applied research. For example, we know of many in-house evaluation studies carried out by these combined methods on the functioning of welfare institutions such as old people's homes, juvenile delinquency treatment projects, and "therapeutic communities" in mental health settings.

Zelditch's argument (1962), and Trow's (1957) with Becker and Geer (1957, 1958), suggests that the need to interrelate data is actually inherent in field methodology, because a field study is not a single method gathering a single kind of information. In particular, the use of informants in relation to observational work is "not only legitimate but absolutely necessary" to investigate complex structures. First, the observer cannot be everywhere at the same time, nor can he be present throughout time. Informants used as "colleagues" can make good this deficit. Second, there will be segments of the structure which the observer cannot penetrate; "there has never been a participant observer study in which the observer acquired full knowledge of all roles and statuses through his own direct observation, and for that matter there never will be such a study by a single observer" (Zelditch 1962, p. 570). The researcher needs either informants or a team of observers.

The test that ethnographers commonly cite for validity is the extent to which different methods that measure common facts produce the same result; a high degree of inter-method or convergent validity is sought. An instance is Falabella's report of a study of Chilean rural migratory workers, the Torrantes:

> I relied heavily on Arias as an informant. His observations are generally confirmed by the information I gathered from my own experiences in the Trail and from interviewing other Torrantes. I gathered further convergent data from recording autobiographies of the Torrantes and from interviewing members of strata surrounding the Torrantes. Arias was very important in the general focus of the research because he allowed me to check my interpretations.... Thus Arias as an informant and participation as a technique seemed to produce reliable information. (Falabella 1981, p. 218)

But the assertion of generality is as important in the formation of an adequate analysis as it is in quality control.

Thus we may refer to Blumer's description of the "generic frame," where frame is taken as a basic structural unit into which other constituents of a whole are fitted. "A frame is generic when the structure or process explicated is chosen and brought to a level of abstraction that makes it generally applicable rather than applicable only in a given institutional realm or ideological debate or other localized concern" (Blumer 1969, p. 129). An example of a report using a generic frame is one of Davis' studies of physical stigma: "the stages through which the relationship between a visibly handicapped person and a physically normal person may move are framed as an instance of a process of deviance disavowal" (Davis 1972, p. 10). By definition, the generic frame that arises from a specific data source can be found in a variety of settings.

In ethnography the analytic claim is not "if a person is presented with stimulus A, he will do B," but "if a person is in situation X, performance Y will be judged proper by members of the culture." As Van Maanen notes, validity testing in this domain is primitive, and ultimately it is the "social test" that counts. Such tests reflect the collective judgment of colleagues. Both conventional and novel expectations of scholarship are involved in the attempt by others to assess the account in terms of previous work and prevailing beliefs about what constitutes proper social science. The fact that this test is imperfect, Van Maanen remarks (1982a, p. 86), "says only that ethnographers, like all other research achievements, are themselves cultural products." Despite his assertion that validity is grounded in "the return trip," the sense of his argument is that the utility of one's analysis to colleagues is as much a criterion as the literal attempt to use ethnographic reports to get by in the same setting.

Despite the frequent assumption that data derived from field research are particularly compatible, the conventional approach to interview data may often be in disjunction from the range of relevances of observational data. A necessary part of the "linking" project is to specify some of the complex considerations that are implicit in our selection, organization, and presentation of a data base. In qualitative research, this is seen as a need to have data that can be assessed by the rules of contextual inference in order to clarify how our observations and interview extracts can be transformed so as to stand for a much larger but invisible set of materials. Cicourel has commented that qualitative researchers seldom acknowledge their limited capacity for processing the rich detail of their materials. The danger is that of reifying the data base, attributing excessive significance to limited segments of data, or drawing on unacknowledged bits of information from other sources of knowledge than the data at hand to the reader. This is not confined to qualitative materials but applies to our use of interviews and questionnaire data. "These activities parallel the way we must elaborate our interpretation of aggregated questionnaire responses, census and demographic materials, and historical texts, in order to endow them with some sense of their consequences for understanding everyday living" (Cicourel 1981, p. 63). Sometimes the researcher's conclusion that something is obvious, clear, and does not require its warrant "displayed" arises from personal observation and other contextual knowledge. Indications of how interpretative summaries of field notes and transcripts are produced are called for.

Glaser and Strauss speak of "theoretical sampling" in the selection of informants, in which who is interviewed, at what stage of research, and in what manner is decided in relation to the researcher's state of knowledge and judgment as to how it could best be extended. The norms of survey interviews and ethnographic interviewing differ in this matter of sampling, and in the fact that in the former the interview is the sole data source whereas in the latter several other contextual data sources are acknowledged. It is a matter of some importance in the interpretation of interview data, as is shown in this account of work on the United States Congress:

> I sometimes appear to rely chiefly upon interviews, but in fact I was living in Washington at the time, spent much of my "free" time in a congressional office, saw a good deal of several congressional assistants and secretaries socially, worked on other matters with several persons actively engaged in relationships with Congress (lobbying and liaison), had participated in a number of congressional campaigns, had read extensively about congressional history and behavior, and had some relevant acquaintance with local politics in several congressional districts. All these factors made my analysis of interviews somewhat credible. As I look back, interviews sometimes acquired meaning from the observations which I often made while waiting in congressional offices.... And, finally, most important of all, it happened that interviews with constituents, lobbyists, congressmen of different views and factions, could be and were checked and re-checked against each other. (Dexter 1970, p. 15)

There is a good deal of difference between the interviews discussed in standard research methods texts and the actual practice of interviews. Many texts emphasize structured interviews. "It is assumed that the interviewer can manipulate the situation and has control over a set list of questions that have been formulated *before* the interview and which are to be *answered* rather then considered, re-phrased, re-ordered, discussed and analyzed" (Burgess 1984, p. 101). Such recipes ape "objectivity" by reducing what is in fact a temporary relationship to a depersonalized question-and-answer session. Researchers such as Wakeford (1981) point out that rather few field studies actually adhere to the structured approach. Unstructured ("informal") or semi-structured interviews are prevalent, partly because of the attraction of allowing the interviewees to develop their answers in their full complexity outside any pre-structuring format. The approach is pitched at achieving proximity to the terms in use in the cultures in which interviewees experience the world and construct meaning. In contemporary practice the approach is, then, closely in harmony with the stock approach of observation methods. Both approaches generate a richness of detail, intimate field relations and resultant problems of "reactivity," a concern with "reflexivity" so that data and research instruments are seen as closely bound, and a great deal of material which may take immense effort to be rendered manageable.

It is conventional to carry out interview work of this sort after a period of orientation by observation. Many follow Zweig's (1948) advice that this style of interview cannot be started without detailed knowledge and an introspective first analysis. Observation is needed before questions can be framed and before people will be prepared to respond in depth. Apart from establishing the interviewer's bona fides, such preparations are necessary if the interviewer is to manage the course of the interview. The interviewer needs to have a grasp of what lines and leads are relevant before s/he can achieve the subtle task of encouraging the interviewee to be expansive on the interesting things but terse on the rest.

With these strong points of contact, it might be assumed that there is a healthy literature on linking data from interviews and observation. This is hardly the case. Before examining how this may be done by reference to empirical examples, we may comment on how interviews can augment observation. Because they are "recognizable" as a social research procedure, interviews can be useful devices to get a first "look" at social settings. Trust and confidence are more important than "controlling" the interview. The interview can be a means to gain entry and to assess the situation for observation. Choosing whether to follow Zweig's advice may depend on the extent of the researcher's existing knowledge of the setting and the nature of the access negotiation.

In his study of the National Front, Nigel Fielding (1982) started with an interview, also using the occasion to get a sense of the reaction of National Front members to his appearance and manner. Success in approaching a candidate in a local election encouraged him to seek interviews with national party officers, which later facilitated overt and covert observation. A side advantage of the interview was the data gained observationally while waiting for the candidate to be available; and, of course, there was also usable material from the interview itself! A similar tack was taken with most of the interviews at party headquarters; most interest was in the surroundings and the events in progress that formed an apparent "backdrop" to the interviews. As Burgess notes (1984, p. 106), interviews also enable access to another kind of closed setting, those which, for reasons of time, place, or situation, are "closed," e.g., the biography or career history of the interviewee. Details of situations which are not directly witnessed are also available, although they should be checked against other sources or at least for their "internal validity."

It is widely assumed that the problem of validity is greater in interview than in observation data, since the data are one step removed from direct experience. The means for checking are to assess the internal consistency of interview data and to seek verification of information through other sources. Where interviews and observation occur together, some data can often be checked against observations. These procedures can be made systematic by establishing a standardized system for assessing the validity of data and the reliability of the source of a particular item. How much validity to assign to information conveyed by an informant also has to be assessed; unreliable informants may pass information which can be checked by, e.g., organizational records. If one accepts that informant reliability and data validity should be considered separately, a two-dimensional system for assessing data is required. In her study of New York police culture, Reuss-Ianni made explicit the assumptions that often underlie discussions of data validity. She assumed that, the closer the fieldworker is to the data, the more certain he is about what he is observing, and she assigned the highest validity score to data gathered where at least one fieldworker was present during the reported activity. When the fieldworkers were not present as participants, lower validity scores were assigned to data gathered by interviewing informants; interview data were coded in three categories according to how careful a check was feasible. "Data which could be checked against standard, available documented sources — complaint reports, precinct statistics, and so on — received the highest score, and where the data came from one source only, we assigned the lowest score" (Reuss-Ianni 1983, p. 134).

The assumptions made in appraising the reliability of informants also need to be made overtly. In the police culture study, the fieldworkers could get a cumulative impression of informant reliability because they were constantly comparing data as they came in. There were several reliability categories. The "always reliable" category was where information from that source was consistently accurate in terms of factual checks or subsequent interviewing; "usually reliable" was where data usually but not always checked out; "reliability unknown" was where it had not been possible to check; and "unreliable" was for informants who on checking were seldom accurate. The rating of data in this way made it possible for Reuss-Ianni to adhere to a rigorous standard. Once reliability and validity scores were assigned to the interview data, the two scores were combined into an index number, and only those units of data that had a reliability-validity index showing that they were corroborated by other informants and were from usually reliable informants, were used.

Observation and Interview Data

The conventional approach to the value of interrelating data from different sources essentially draws on principles for reading a text (e.g., a historical or literary work) which preceded development of social science methodology. It is assumed that "meaning" is accessible "on the surface" of the discourse. A further assumption is that a method to evaluate the veracity of the discourse is immediately available by comparing what appears there with what appears in other sources in print. Suspicion and the need to back up one's arguments is part of the human condition, but consistency can be a powerful argument in favor of an interpretation. As is obvious, it can also be a powerful influence in encouraging a static scholarship that resists novel interpretations. This criterion is all that one is getting at in the concept of "external validity," which holds that valid conclusions are recognized by their being replicated across other subjects (persons), places, times, and "operationalizations" of the institution or procedure under study.

Generalization is an object of both some quantitative and some qualitative studies. Quantitative research oriented to this standard must show that similar results obtain with other samples or other measures of the same variables, while qualitative research has to show that similar results occur in other settings. We have already discussed McCleary's study of parole officers. It is a study which does not rest with asserting the generality of the reporting decisions among Chicago officers, or parole officers generally, but claims that the processes pertain generally to social service agencies (McCleary 1978, p. 171). Since replication is seldom done, the qualitative researcher must show that the process studied is similar to those that occur in other settings and among other people. It is a big assertion, and its plausibility hinges on the monothetic classification procedure of piling up numerous points of similarity between the settings/persons being compared.

In many cases, the researcher claims to be less interested in the site than in the form of interaction. Such claims can be rather broad; if we are comparing interaction processes we may feel there are at least a few ways in which virtually any interaction is similar to any other. It is also not clear at what point exceptions undermine the case for "similarity." How many divergent features can be tolerated? Strictly, monothetic classifications call for a new class if there is even one. An instance of this assertion is Kidder's study of hypnotism workshops:

> The hypnotists negotiated several aspects of reality with their subjects.... I regard this as a study of negotiated realities and consider it similar to other studies of the social construction of reality. The process I studied is like the process that Becker studied in his report on individuals who become marijuana

users, and like the process Scheff studied in his report of therapists' and patients' negotiations.... I am less concerned with generalizing to other hypnosis workshops than I am with generalizing to other situations where two or more parties negotiate definitions of what happened and who was responsible. (Kidder 1981, pp. 251–252)

The consistency claim depends on what it is that the study is supposed to have discovered, but it seems that the grander the claimed discovery conceptually, the harder it is to determine whether it is warranted by consistency. "I wished to generalize to other phenomena which may appear very different on the surface but which share the stages and the negotiations that I described," wrote Kidder (1981).

This is a common desire, but it means that in practice the comparison often turns on the abstracted versions of the concept and not on the concept's "working" in application to the microscopic details of the settings from which the concepts are derived. "I contend that the external validity of my findings depends on their similarity to findings from very different settings, such as learning to become a marijuana user or learning to accept someone else's definition of one's ailment" (Kidder 1981, p. 252). Concepts are "validated" by the selection of points of similarity and the burying of points of divergence. This kind of thing goes on in seminars and even in the literature. The studies which are most open to it are those that do not claim causality but present themselves as "suggestive" or "invitational."

An effort to interrelate data from different sources in the same study can partly meet the problem by tightening the base from which the concept emerges. But the interrelated data themselves rely on an assertion about similarity. Interview and observational data must be assumed to be of a comparable "level," to possess similar levels of "reactivity" and "artefact," and to be similar in other ways if they are to serve this purpose. This contrasts with the dissimilarity of non-random sources of error central to triangulation's hypothesis-"winnowing." We do not think, as some do, that this means that the use of different sources of data cannot further the end of establishing the bounds of validity. However, it does mean that the comparability of the data to be interrelated must be established as rigorously as the concept that is built on such a base. If we do not replicate, we are obliged to work inductively, so that we infer similarity of "processes, structure or meaning." Claims as to similarity thus rest on inference, not similarities that are "visible," and so external validity is an absolute standard which can never be finally achieved (Campbell and Stanley 1963, p. 5).

Like Kidder's work, and Becker's, the study of the National Front revolved around the various meanings given to deviant behavior by the parties involved. The idea that deviance is not a quality of the act but the attribution of a label to the act directs attention to the process by which meaning and significance are accorded. Some sociologists have used the analysis of the observable facets of such behaviors to infer the hidden, subjective motivation of behavior, deviance being seen as a political struggle between those having different interpretations of meaning. Political deviance is important here analytically because it not only involves divergence from "normal" views but is explicitly articulated. The case of political deviance offers the prospect of data about the way individuals consider action in light of beliefs about ends and commitment to the demands of ideologies.

To get at such matters, a naturalistically oriented study has to claim achievement of such proximity to members as to enable belief-oriented decision-making to become accessible. We have seen the standard devices already: long acquaintance by staying in the field for a respectable time, and, ultimately, the claim to have constructed in the "interior" of the researcher a false, setting-specific self, from which intuitive base the researcher can work out how members think about such things as joining in assaults on opponents. Initially it was important to decide what degree of penetration of the National Front would be necessary. A review of the very large literature on the extreme Right revealed that much existing work had involved a very low level of researcher-subject interaction. For example, a study of the Minutemen included the statement that, "since I already had access to transcripts of public addresses by Minutemen leaders as well as to their confidential directives to members, I decided that the very slight probability of gaining new information by interview was not worth the expenditure of time that would be involved" (Albares 1968, pp. 3–4).

A study of the operationalization of an ideology in routine member practices needed a closer approach than this, and led to the choice of a participant observation methodology. An initial request to interview a party official provided first contact with a National Directorate member who became a key informant, and with whom a relationship of trust developed over a period of two years. He proved an invaluable contact in arranging further interviews, attendance at branch meetings, marches and demonstrations, and introductions to other members. Meanwhile, covert observation of activities of local branches was taking place in several regions. One branch was chosen for extensive covert observation.

The criterion of intimate participation as a measure of "adequacy" in the naturalistic approach made me acutely aware of my evolving stance towards members. Although with some I maintained a formal researcher role and with others a friendly near-convert status, with all of them I tried to project a sympathetic attitude to the culture of which they were members. I wrote that "this involved an instrumental and temporary suspension of my own political views" (Fielding 1981, p. 8). I paid much attention to my gradually developing relationship of trust, and its limits, in the separate field log I kept based on Bruyn's "subjective criteria of adequacy." I found the device of feeding back interview transcripts and some field notes, minus my own analytic coding, a useful one in cultivating "trust," but I felt that the primary device remained the preservation of an "open and sympathetic attitude."

I began to experience a puzzling sensation; I knew of many brutal and repellent acts committed by members, yet in their routine dealings on their own ground they seemed entirely "normal."

As one gains knowledge of the personality of NF supporters... one is impressed by their (public) restraint and apparent moderation. One wishes to "appreciate," not to be converted, yet once the key aspects of their position are grasped it seems rationally accomplished. This is the public face. The National Front outside election time, and in the actions of its supporters when not mindful of the need for impression-management, has preserved a brutal attitude towards opposing groups. (Fielding 1981, pp. 8–9)

Analytic use was eventually made of this disjunction between the members on their best behavior (with the identified researcher in an overt role) and the members involved in political violence (in cases witnessed in covert observation). It is sometimes said of Hitler's followers that they too were "ordinary, decent folk," and to me then the disjunction betrayed the tyranny of mediocrity. But a quite different point could have been made. The disjunction could have been used to show the way in which members were producing a performance for the researcher, and to discount the wisdom of a literal treatment of data from such occasions.

Participant observation is particularly associated with the naturalistic perspective, as we have noted. There is no necessary connection; after all, the essential procedures of observation are commonly used by investigative journalists, those engaged in industrial espionage, and spies. Douglas has latterly argued for an investigative rather than a naturalistic perspective in sociological observations. The National Front study did diverge from a straightforward "appreciative" stance in one respect. Observers applying a naturalistic perspective stress the need to study groups with which one feels some affinity because the approach hinges on rapport, seen as a means of maximizing "trust" and hence access to "the facts." Lofland (1971), for example, suggests that researchers ask themselves whether they genuinely like the group's members before choosing observational methods. Sociologists using this approach have tended to study groups with which they have some sympathy, e.g., blacks, homosexuals, the radical Left. In choosing the National Front, I was choosing an "uncongenial" group. I felt it was a good exercise to apply similar techniques to the study of a group with which few sociologists of any kind have sympathy.

From the outset, my notion of "appreciation" could not be a simple one. I could not simply render a sympathetic portrait; and, with my interest in ideology in view, I could not rest with an emic analysis, merely treating formally the concepts in use by members. By regarding their beliefs as ideology at all, I was implicitly accepting that there could be other beliefs and that their "fit" to the real world would be an issue. But there was enough of an appreciative stance left to make the disjunction jarring between those I came to know and what I knew they did. The need to interrelate data seemed mandatory once I predicated that there was more to the group than its formal ideology and formal organization. The moment I accepted the need for covert as well as overt work, the concepts of formal and informal organization, and of the articulation of the two, came with it. The intention to relate expressed beliefs to those routinely held in itself necessitated such a methodology. Arguing that it was necessary to specify the interrelations between beliefs (informal, lay), ideology (formal, party officials), and action (the arena of their interrelation), I attended to the "linkages... between the psychic organization of individuals, the formal organization of the party, and the formal ideology" (Fielding 1981, p. 11).

While I was concerned with the development of members' alternative interpretations of political reality, the *verstehen* methodology made for certain definite constraints. The case for the method focuses on the need to respect the integrity of the subject, to allow the subjects to give their own account by responding to sociologically significant questions, and to gain data from lay members as well as from official pronouncements. Yet at the same time I was assessing these beliefs for their "fit" to "reality." The task of exposing the constituent parts of a belief system suffers the holistic criticism. The resulting analysis is likely to produce a mechanical impression of ideology, for how can one appreciate without being merged with the subject of appreciation? If one sets out to make a rational reconstruction of an irrational belief system, a totalitarian belief system which puts prime stress on feeling and "thinking with the blood," one's efforts are doomed. In a sense, the moment one succeeds (in the production of a rational reconstruction), one fails.

There was a second constraint. One of my concerns was the motivation behind political deviance, where I argued that the origin of sympathy for the NF was in pre-existing moral, non-political attitudes, such as are betrayed in ethnic stereotyping. But the fieldwork precluded specification of "why" people join because by definition I was dealing with those who were already members. The naturalistic rejoinder is weak; the observer can only assert that he knows his subject. "My data only permit me to suggest that a link exists, and it is a suggestion based on long and thorough exposure to a wide range of members" (Fielding 1981, p. 13). This is something that has to be taken on trust, particularly where replication is even less likely than usual owing to the hostility of the group to outsiders and especially researchers. Because of this, the only alternative to an intensive concern with assessing the procedural mechanics of fieldwork (did the author stay in the culture for ages, see hundreds of people, etc.) is to demonstrate points by bringing several different sources of data to bear on them.

Data Combined

To illustrate, let us take the case of the security consciousness of members. Pertaining to an extremist group in active confrontation with black, left-wing, and anti-fascist groups, the data would be expected to reflect a degree of awareness of threat. Since differences in this, involvement in political action, and internalization of key ideological points were noted, a distinction between "ordinary" and "active" members was suggested. While the brunt of political action is by activists, ordinary members support what they see as the heroism of the activists in defending the party against its enemies.

One important aspect of security was the way the NF dealt with harassment by opponents. Data were cited which show that one of its responses is to seek good relations with the police, who are in any case thought by members to be more sympathetic to the NF than to their opponents. The data were from conversations with members while accompanying them on marches in a covert role. But it is not only harassment at public events which poses a threat. Physical description from observation was used here. The NF headquarters was the subject; it was entered by a heavily bolted and chained, windowless door. Members were instructed always to use the spyhole before admitting anybody, and to keep the door chained on first opening it. (In my experience they always did this.) The building was a terraced (row) house bearing neither name nor number, and its facade was encased in bolted sheets of corrugated iron. The stairs from the ground floor were monitored by a two-way mirror.

Apart from physical description, conversational data were also applied to the theme. It was noted that quite frequently the HQ staff adopted a secretive attitude. On one occasion I asked a party officer how many people worked there: "We are not really going to say that. That is not for release" (interview, 7 June 1974). When I asked on another occasion what office hours the party chairman kept I was told: "This is not released. You can see why, a lot of people would like that information."

These data applied to active members, indeed party officers. My interest was also in the degree of security consciousness of ordinary members. At the time, branch members showed a continual concern with security. A week after a riot in which an anti-fascist had been killed and a police officer fatally injured in a melee outside an NF meeting, I attended a branch meeting where a South London member told the branch organizer, "If we use coaches at our next march they will have to be properly looked after. We should put somebody on the coaches while they're parked, put enough security on the coaches to make sure that when we come back there aren't no nasty surprises under the seat. You know as well as I do the security at some branches is terrible, and we don't want to find something under our seats" (field notes, 25 June 1974). This seemed to be important data; not only did it show an understandably high level of awareness, it indicated variation within the movement (some branches were not careful to check for bombs). The organizer replied that, following the riot (outside London's Conway Hall), the NF had learnt by bitter experience how to take care of security. "At Conway Hall they [HQ] had a staff, well, I call it a staff, they had 65 tough blokes, and they checked everybody coming in, and before the meeting they were all through the hall and outside, and checked to make sure that no one was lurking to bash anyone on the head."

Immediately following this statement came another comment that addressed one of my analytic concerns—qualifiers on commitment and variations in involvement in political action — and seemed to carry more force because it arose of its own accord. The activist to whom the organizer had replied, a burly young working-class man, declared: "I shall turn up anyway, no matter what the security, and so will me mates, but I'm thinking of the women and children. They'll want to be on the march and we want to be sure they're all right. Because the Oxford lot are a right lot, a good lot, but you know what I mean." He meant they were one of the aggressive branches who were careless about security. The organizer concluded: "You've got my guarantee, this you can rely on, we're good on security. The Front knows how to defend itself and you can trust it will be taken care of." The branch secretary then suggested organizing a defense course for members along with training in first aid.

Another analytic theme had been the low level of involvement of ordinary members in the rather dull routine of meetings. It thus seemed especially important that the only enthusiastic response during the meeting which involved all those present was this discussion of security. Together, the data on the fortress-like headquarters, the secretiveness of HQ officials, the aggressive response to the frightening events of the week before (especially for those inside the building surrounded by rioting anti-NF demonstrators), and the involvement of ordinary members as well as activists in planning future marches were used to support a notion of the unifying nature of questions of party security:

> It is here that the concern of the ideology with conflict and the demands of the patriotic stance are most easily perceived as translatable into demands for action by the members. It is action which is noble and dramatic, unlike the plodding tasks of electoral politics. Perhaps the dramatic semiotic aspect of the action is of more import to members than the physical conflict it often entails. (Fielding 1981, p. 38)

Of course, there is no way of knowing the answer to this latter speculative point. But it was intended that the data presented in the text that led up to it rendered this necessary part of the case more plausible.

Lofland has written of the need to achieve an "interpenetrated" analysis, one in which, ideally, the "generic, novel, elaborated and eventful frame that grows out of immersion in the natural setting is, as a consequence of emergence and development from the qualitative data, also *interpenetrated* by it" (1974, p. 110). By taking "security" as a frame, several different components of analysis could be addressed consequently or in propinquity. Texts built in this way seek for the happy state in which frame and data co-exist as one whole, each depending on the other for the interest the reader has in either. Interpenetrated reports are marked by a minute and continual *alternation* between data and frame-elements.

Data in Conflict

What to do when items of data are in conflict is less obvious than what to do when one can find some coherent binding thread to link data from different sources. The problem is particularly trying when data from one methodology contradict data from another. The issue of NF membership and social class posed this problem. Lipset stated the conventional status politics explanation of affiliation to the extreme Right: "fascism is basically a middle class movement representing a protest against both capitalism *and* socialism, big business *and* big unions" (1959, p. 349). I felt this was a terribly crude category, which ignored the role of the party's ideology and its function as a primary community for members. Along with Bell (1963), Lipset and Raab (1970) subdivided class groups in the extreme Right into traditional middle class and new urban middle class, but had problems explaining the involvement of the working class.

The data on class support for Nazism are more comprehensive than those on class support for the American extreme Right, and they treat support as coming from intermediate (lower middle-class) strata. In the 1930s, almost half the registered Nazis were employees (chiefly clerical) or self-employed people, shopkeepers, and craftspeople. Farmers, petty officials, and teachers were strongly supportive. The most notably under-represented groups were industrial workers; at 50 percent of the population, they accounted for but 30 percent of party membership. Nazism was weakest in big cities, industrial areas, and strongly Catholic rural areas (Allen 1965).

While these generalizations were supported powerfully by quantitative data, I felt they were open to qualification. Initially, this reflected uneasiness with the analysis at a purely conceptual level. The problem with the analysis was the mechanical notion of the link between class groups in which support was concentrated and the appeal of the ideology. In the American literature, the reactionary ideology was depicted as being focused against competing groups in the social structure, and its appeal was simply as a means of opposing rising status groups or "East Coast intellectuals." Why this potential should be realized by those from one background and not from another when both are equally persuaded by the racialist component of the ideology was unclear. The analysis of Nazism improved on this by noting the selective appeal of the ideology and the way the Nazis maximized it by responding to the perceived needs of class groups hostile to them. To this could be added the finding, from research on postwar European reactionary groups, that there were geographically distinct cultural enclaves nurturing their own tradition of Rightism. A sophisticated analysis would therefore interrelate class background with geographical situation and with the applicability of ideology in terms of its "spread" across the range of an individual's experience.

However, I did not want to argue that NF support comes from one particular combination of causes. In C. T. Husbands' (1975) comparison of constituencies where the NF vote exceeded 5 percent in the 1974 elections, at least two broad patterns emerged. Although the NF did do better in areas of high immigrant population, in London this was chiefly in areas of economic decline and population loss, and which returned Labour candidates. Thus, "the coincidence of large Labour majorities and exceptionally low turnout — occurring as they did in some of London's most depressed inner-city areas — suggests an electorate that is mainly working-class and from parts of which... the Front gathered support based on protest motives" (Husbands 1975, p. 405). In contrast, in the Midlands constituencies where the NF did well, the local economy was prosperous and the "immigrant" population consisted chiefly of relatively high-status Indian/Pakistani people. Their arrival, Husbands commented, "caused severe strain to the indigenous white population." Thus, the NF seemed to appeal to at least two forms of reaction: "immigrant backlash" and "socio-economic malaise."

I still had some qualifiers to add, notably that there was variation in class membership by branch, with some branches dominated by the retired middle class, others dominated by middle-class and professional people, and others mainly by working-class members. But on the strength of observation, all I could go on was subjective assessment; in covert observation I could hardly grill people about their occupations, their father's occupations, and so on. As to the interviews, all I could get was the "party line" — the NF was a "classless" movement. My findings remained largely subjective assessments based on unsystematic observation, literature (renegade and ex-members' accounts were especially important but also dubious), and "a galaxy of no doubt subliminal sensations." I felt there was warrant in such typifications as "the general spirit of the movement is aggressively working class," but, if pressed, I could only repeat the few indiscreet remarks about class which party officers let drop in my presence. For example, one official told me that he did not see his own affiliation as a product of the direct effect of immigration. He was from a middle-class family and had never lived in an area with many immigrants. He nevertheless said: "I see the NF as a product of socio-economic pressures." He would "rather convert Reds than some of these Tories" because the Tories were so steeped in class interests. Nor was the NF yet a mass movement, but "we do have a popular base," being particularly strong among the "skilled working class" (Fielding 1981, p. 50). Such data were somewhat equivocal.

Faced with the fact that I could not support a critique by the kind of data I had, I switched to a "suggestive" emphasis. I presented a series of case studies in which I attempted a presentation of "types" in which class, "measured 'objectively' and subjectively," was "an important but not exclusive facet." Accepting that class was a useful label, I argued that one should still be aware that referring to the "upper-class member" included not only those of peak income and hereditary title but also those whose subjective orientation to class was to the style associated with such groups. Rather than class, I dealt with "social types" (see Klapp 1964). The term denoted not simply an occupational category or a psychologically complex description, but emphasized "outstanding features so as to enable the identification of individuals for people studying the milieu" (Fielding 1981, p.

50). The case studies included a certain amount of incidental detail, whose explicit purpose was to invest the social "types" with some life, but also added some of the contradictions and subtleties which I was aware of ethnographically and which prevented my satisfaction with any simple typification of members by reference to gross indicators of social class.

My key informant was offered as an example of a "lower middle-class male activist." However, in writing the description it was apparent to me how difficult it would be to regard him as "typical"; indeed, it seemed that, if one knew as much as I had learnt about *any* member of the activist group, the idea of "typicality" would be subverted. McCalden was an Ulsterman who trained as a teacher of social studies; he was well-traveled, and had numerous interests outside politics, notably animal welfare. He had a pleasant, slightly diffident manner, a sharp mind, and a fascination with detail. His father had been a signalman in Belfast but had been made redundant. McCalden went to a grammar school, an above-average form of schooling in the state system, and he found academic subjects more involving than sport. At school he was "always in the debating societies, drama club. When I was about 15 I got into Maoism, and I bought a copy of the 'Thoughts of Chairman Mao.' It wasn't easy to find a copy then, he wasn't popular yet. I went round the school advocating the policies, the nationalism of Mao. It was just a fad. Everyone goes through it. Some NF members used to be Nazis at school, then grew out of it" (interview, 6 May 1974).

Such details seemed to undermine at once the summary of the salient features of biography by reference to marginal social status; here was man as an active agent, not a passive vessel into which "meanings" were poured by demographic factors and outside influences. McCalden's case suggested that the route to political commitment was anything but direct, an idea that closely informed my overall analysis of affiliation and adherence; I argued from the observation that "progress is halting and involves numerous false starts and near-involvements." I became sensitive to any indications of failures of resolve, second-thoughts, or expressions of ambivalence and tolerance for it on the part of members.

This idea was underpinned by another idea derived from theory outside conventional political sociology. There was warrant in the sociology of deviance and studies of social movements to argue that people do "shop around" before cementing their affiliation to deviant in-groups. I had heard stories of people who had passed from one end of the political spectrum to the other where the extremism of the group with which they had experimented was the only common thread, and I expected to encounter people whose orientation had originally been to the extreme Left. It seemed to me that such people were directly touched by politics; and, having broken ranks with the party their biography made most available to them, it was unpredictable which group would ultimately gain their adherence.

Thus, because I was studying the relatively unusual case of people for whom the rectitude of their political orientation was important, it would indeed be strange if the gross factors that explain routine (low-level) commitment for most people was the most important point with them. The problem was that, if I had the additional knowledge I had about the people in my typology for, say, a "representative" sample of the voting population, the conventional status/class argument might begin to look very unconvincing; but because I did not, my critique was necessarily limited to a small group of activists. Although I could remark, of McCalden, that in many ways his traits could be considered typical of an individual adhering to an extreme Left position, I could only conclude that "such contradictions are salutary in correcting the public stereotypes that grow up around the participants in the public arena."

While the "class" argument about membership illustrates the potential and constraints of qualitative data, and the points at which quantitative data can make the analysis more powerful, there are a number of points where the interrelation of different types of qualitative data can help resolve contested interpretations. One such was the involvement of party officials in political violence. Covert observation had its limits here, and additional sources of data were imperative. At the same time, eclecticism of sources did not excuse efforts to establish the veracity of reports culled from internal party documents, its official publications, renegade-member accounts, discussions with opponents, and press and police information. In the nature of the subject some information presented was contentious; some was from sources which may have been considered dubious or politically motivated. I sought to identify it as such. Where cases were essential to the argument, I presented examples which I believed to be valid, but I also included cases where NF involvement was only strongly suspected, or where only a single source was available. Crucial points were supported by the weight of evidence from as many sources as possible, and I included only those whose veracity was established to the best of my knowledge.

Libel considerations constrained reference to information about informal but functional links between the NF and those who may be inclined to commit political violence. The official line was that involvement of NF members in any such incidents was in defense against opponents who had taken the first step, although there was also frequent reference to the way that the mere presence of opponents was in itself "provocation." Nevertheless, a great deal more circumstantial evidence was available than it was possible to publish, and this increased the value of any direct reference in official party literature to involvement. The rarity of NF reports of attacks on opponents made the cynical tone of this one especially important. When an NF official was attacked by an opponent on a march in Portsmouth, the opponent "somehow managed to collapse to the ground and was accidentally trampled underfoot by successive ranks of marchers. When police finally managed to drag his body out of the gutter he was completely stunned and bleeding from the throat" (*Britain First* 1976). In another case, an explicit report appeared of an incident in which the then-chairman of the party had organized an assault on members of the International Marxist Group; the report could have been considered as describing a normally covert action which had been made overt as part of the increasing aggressiveness of the party.

It is fair to say that many of those involved in the study of racist political movements in the 1970s found such incidents an adequate reflection of the party's nature. Yet I was aware of cases where the NF leadership had restrained members from precipitate action. I saw these as cases of the attempt to manage the impression publicly given of the party; but whatever the motive, there were cases which did not fit an unambiguous "bully boy" depiction. A letter from the Deputy Chairman to a supporter read in part:

> The Humphrey [sic] Berkeley gig at the South African Society sounds like fun. But I think we will have to be on our very best behaviour, as I do not think it would do to cause a riot at one of the Society's meetings. I think a dozen or so of our more thoughtful members would do better than 50 rowdy types, even though Berkeley does deserve a really strong ragging.

This was followed by reference to a case which I felt established the NF's cynical "tactical" sense in adopting a stance in relation to particular incidents. Evidence was available linking the NF to a series of fire-bomb attacks on immigrant-owned property in London in 1973. While I had to note that there was a difficulty in separating those allegedly undertaken with NF involvement from those done by local residents in situations of racial harassment, I felt a published reference to it by Webster was indicative of the NF's determination to extract advantage from such cases by denying direct involvement while representing such action as the understandable, justifiable, and even inevitable response of white residents under pressure in their "own" land:

> The NF, quite obviously, has no truck with such activity.... But if White people... who have not been yet brought into contact with the NF have engaged from time to time in a guerrilla war struggle against the Black invaders of their Borough as a result of rage and frustration caused by the assaults, intimidations, discriminations, and indignities which they and their relatives have had to bear, then the politicians and the Community Relations workers have only got themselves to blame. (*Spearhead* 1974)

The inclusion of the NF's account of the cases enabled the cases to be mentioned while establishing that, even in print, the NF did not trouble to condemn such action unequivocally. This point was immediately followed by an account of data from covert observation in which, in a conversation with a branch activist, I was given details of a series of meetings of an extreme Left group he had infiltrated.

> "In fact I went to an IS meeting at the ____. You know, they always hold their meetings there, well, upstairs, and then come down to the bar. The meetings are always at 8." On his last visit he "wasn't wearing a lapel pin or anything but

somehow they just knew I was NF, they just picked me out." (Fielding 1981, p. 181)

He then began to press me about my own support for the NF. This information was related to reports in internal party literature of infiltration by NF members in a number of groups. Again, the point was to establish the consideration of courses of action by the party on the basis of tactical advantage.

Wherever I could treat an incident by reports from those involved alongside official party reports, outside media reports, and my own observation, I did so. The idea was to provide text that was an adequate description based on all the data available to me, while recognizing that I could not avoid mediating such description, if only by evaluating the quality of items of information from different sources. This descriptive project was warranted by the consciously "social scientific" (rather than political) aim of the study, and by the absence of any social science literature at all on the NF at this time. My intention to render a descriptive, if not a "balanced" account, earned me censure among other scholars in ethnic and racial studies (Miles 1981; Fielding 1982b).

The "appreciative" stance was the chief problem here; social scientists seemed used to deriving their concerns from the literature but not from those they studied. My interest in the fit between beliefs and action in support of beliefs required both that I get as good a descriptive base of party action as possible, and that I continually work from beliefs as they are formally expressed in ideological statements, to the informal organization of beliefs as they are mirrored or refracted in the everyday discourse of members. For example, the conviction that "all decent people agree" with NF policies is constantly encountered and is crucial in evaluating the significance to the member of being in an extremist party. It suggests that the only reason all decent ordinary folk do not join is ignorance of the party's nature, or apathy. At one point the ideology seeks to establish its difference from the other, "corrupt" parties, while at this point it seeks to establish legitimacy by denying that its beliefs are extraordinary, let alone extreme. It is a stance which permits members to comfort themselves with the thought that they are not extreme in belief, only more honest than the mass.

To pursue this argument, I set out extracts from ideological statements and interviews with officials in juxtaposition with declarations of belief by ordinary supporters. I asked McCalden whether the coming to power of an NF government would still leave the task of changing the way of thinking of the British people. He replied: "No, because it's government that needs to change, not the people. The majority of the public do agree with our policies. We get so many letters, we've had so many this campaign, but even now many say they are for the NF but they can't vote for us this time because we have no chance. They still throw away their vote" (interview, 18 October 1974). Chairman Tyndall gave the same interpretation. All decent people agreed with NF policies "at heart," but failed to vote NF because they thought it futile.

The party everywhere declared its faith in the average citizen; the Ulster NF's paper "hopes to reflect the pro-British loyalty of the average Ulsterman," while James Doyle, an NF supporter, insisted: "I said years ago what Enoch Powell says today, and I believe 90 percent of the British people support this view." George Wright, a former NF candidate, declared: "You can call us extreme right-wing if you like, but I'd say we were middle-of-the-road. We embrace all types of people except coloured" (*Sunday Times*, 20 June 1976). A woman at an NF election meeting approached the stewards concerning demonstrators outside, saying: "Get out there and smash that bleedin' wog filth. It's a bloody disgrace them and that Red scum out there chanting at respectable people like us." The contrast between the numbers of people who ought to support a group which allegedly appeals to the "ordinary decent Briton" and its actual membership presented a problem which was resolved by attempts to qualify the meaning of "consensus" and, more powerfully, by recourse to conspiracy theory.

There were also instances where the different sources of data were not treated cumulatively but used to identify points of dissonance. One such was over the degree and nature of affective returns from attending the Remembrance Day march, where the official ceremony for Britain's war dead is followed on the same site by an NF ceremony. A letter I received from a branch treasurer asserted the importance of the event to the party: "I hope you enjoy the occasion — I need hardly say, *we* all look forward to it enormously — if anyone has any doubt at all about the National Front, they have only to see the Remembrance Day 'turn-out' and that will convince them for all time" (Fielding 1981 p. 171). However, it seemed clear when I attended the event that it was the march rather than the Cenotaph service which had the greatest hold on members. Many members seemed to pay scant attention to the service, and no one seemed greatly moved. Neither could the rally afterwards be considered the focus of members' attention. Numbers had dwindled from 4,000 to 1,200 by the time the rally began. The majority of this crowd were to be served by hired buses, and in fact most of those left were a captive audience because without attending the rally they could not find their bus.

What, then, did the letter mean? Was the treasurer simply out-of-touch? Observations on the coach ride there and back, the march to the service, the service itself, and the rally suggested that the NF branch is a group that celebrates its collective identity on relatively few occasions. Remembrance Day was the principal one of these, and attention concentrated on the turn-out on the initial march, which is widely used as a barometer of the party's current support. This is reinforced by the fact that this is the only day of the year when every NF member and every regional branch can be expected to be similarly engaged. It was not the content of the event (the service, speeches at the rally, etc.) that was important, but its form. It was an "occasion" which had a valuable symbolic role in binding ordinary members and recruits, and affirming commitment by a show of strength. For once, those belonging to this fringe movement outnumbered all others; in a sense, the NF thus "captured" the setting of its demonstration, with all the official authority of the Cenotaph site. Further, the commemoration of the war dead being free of partisan overtones, the members' need to feel that they express common values was satisfied.

In light of this argument for "symbolic" returns, my case for the nature of commitment needed further specification. I was increasingly reliant on a distinction between "activists" and "ordinary" members. I put this contrast strongly when I reviewed the "sacrifices" made by members as an index of commitment. Sacrifices included time and money spent on the party's behalf, as well as involvement in all kinds of political action and consequent trouble with opponents and the law. Members' preparedness to defend themselves and party property meant that activists had to face the fact they could be killed as part of their political activity. As I was to discover, this ultimate sacrifice was no flight into melodramatic fantasy.

Such considerations even play on the minds of ordinary members. On the Remembrance Day march, a man told me his wife always tried to dissuade him from marching despite her own conversion to the NF. The NF literature on the difficulty of the party's struggle and the evil of its opponents played their part in preparing members for physical danger. McCalden replied unhesitatingly "Yes, certainly" to the question of whether he would use force against an opponent if he thought it vital to the cause.

> There is no way you can exist without using force. Your physical presence somewhere involves violence. You are being violent just as much by standing in someone's way, by blocking a doorway, for example, as if you were to attack someone. We in the National Front certainly have no qualms about defending ourselves. (Fielding 1981, p. 187)

McCalden's commitment was proved to me by an incident in October 1974. On our way to lunch one day he told me, " We had an amusing incident here [HQ] a couple of days ago." A parcel had been delivered of which they were suspicious; parcel bombs were common at this time. No one else in the office would open it, and he volunteered. He stood in the corridor so that if he heard a ticking he could throw it away from himself. He opened the wrapping, and found a margarine tub with a note saying, "This is what you are." He gingerly opened it; the tub was filled with maggots. He added, "They thought this would be an effective blast in favor of the left-wing cause" (Fielding 1981, p. 188). The cynical attitude of the hardened activist did not reduce my feeling that it took courage to deal with the suspect parcel.

My knowledge of my informant and of the other HQ staff suggested that McCalden was not merely being foolhardy, or fabricating the story. One may still challenge such cases; I had not, after all, been present. However, there are cases in which members themselves orient to a matter of analytic concern, striking positions according to the dynamics of some novel event oblivious to the presence of the investigator. I have already noted data bearing on the increasing aggressiveness of the party against opponents. Covert attendance at the Remembrance Day rally revealed data of key importance. The Deputy Chairman's speech represented a new departure for the NF senior leadership in explicitly calling for physical action against opponents. At one point, with anger in his voice and a deliberate intonation, he said: "If the powers-that-be are going to show that they are going to use their influence against us, then I say to you that the time has come, when he confronts us at our meetings and in the streets, to SMASH OUR ENEMY TO A PULP!" (Fielding 1981, pp. 128–129). It was so marked and virulent that it became a point of general discussion. Members discussed the speech on the coach as we returned to the branch. They said it was a new departure. One suggested: "Didn't you think it was a bit strong?" But other activists agreed it was justified (p. 189).

It was evident that party publications then introduced a new sarcasm into their reports of NF involvement in violence. At a disrupted branch meeting the party reported that "The NF activists ejected the red rabble by use of the tried and trusted East London methods of the boot and fist" (*Spearhead* 1975). Of their intervention in the 1976 "Bloody Sunday" IRA demonstration, they wrote:

> The sight of this atrocity-supporting rabble... was just too much for some of our lads, who, with their magnificent Union Jacks flying, were unable to resist making a charge.... Some of our lads (their outrage was understandable) managed to find a gap in the thin police line and, despite being outnumbered 10 to 1, advanced into the middle of the alien mob.... The same enthusiasm and more pre-planning should make next year's "Bloody Sunday" demo. the last ever in London. (*Spearhead* 1976)

The advantage of data in which members' own discourse addresses concerns of interest to the researcher is that, faithfully reported, it comes as close as possible to avoiding problems of reactivity and reflexivity. As we will argue below, this can be particularly valuable in policy-oriented research in service organizations.

The work on the National Front pursued a naturalistic methodology, contrasted by Blumer with the conventional stance of the quantitative researcher:

> In short, one would have to take the role of the actor and see his world from his standpoint. This methodological approach stands in contrast to the so-called objective approach so dominant today, namely that of viewing the actor and his action from the perspective of an outside, detached observer.... The actor acts towards his world on the basis of how he sees it and not on the basis of how that world appears to the outside observer. (Blumer 1966, p. 542)

At the close of his comment, Blumer is referring to the subjectivity or "perspectival" problem. Clearly, the status of the members' and the researcher's understanding is at issue. We may briefly consider an approach which brings this perspectival problem to center-stage and which seeks to turn it from a limitation to a source of analytic insight.

We may consider an example in which the inevitability of different versions is actually turned to analytic use. Triangulation often means combining complementary methods, but it can also refer to using a number of data sources, achieving a sense of a number of accounts of events. Cicourel's study of the acquisition and use of language in primary school involved the collection of several accounts of classroom activity by interviewing teachers and children about audio and video recordings made in class. This technique of "indefinite triangulation" aimed to show how various interpretations of objective events can be assembled from people having different physical, temporal, and biographically situated experience of the situation (Cicourel et al. 1974). One may criticize the model of social action, which suggests that data such as interview extracts can be taken literally or at face value, any error in measurement or bias being remedied statistically. There is no warrant to *assume* that circumstances will match to the extent necessary to enable comparison of data across numerous respondents; any such inference must be warranted empirically.

As with ethnomethodological work, the "accounts" argument can be helpful in quality control, used selectively. The accounts argument holds that it is misguided to attempt to furnish descriptions and explanations of what actually happens. The goal is unrealizable because people in different contexts give contradictory accounts of phenomena. The researcher can only produce a coherent, single picture by arbitrarily selecting accounts produced in some contexts while ignoring those produced in others. In extreme form, it is said that we can therefore never know anything sociological about people's beliefs and practices. The sociologist can only switch to the analysis of the nature of the discourse through which people provide their diverse accounts of reality.

It is asserted that this makes interpretative problems recede. But does it? Skeptics may not agree that a resort to discourse analysis avoids the kind of interpretative work necessitated by attempts to describe and explain social action. Those things of interest here, such as "interpretative regularities," do not make themselves apparent merely by the passive, inductive inspection of transcribed interviews. Given that "the facts" do not "speak for themselves" and that all knowledge is socially contingent, a point this position makes central to its critique, it is hardly likely that this form of analysis is itself exempt from these principles. But it does offer a procedure of some value in assessing the quality of interview data and conversation witnessed in fieldwork. Indeed, when interpretations made in discourse analysis conflict, analysts are forced into the same reasoning that ethnographers use to back up their cases: attention to the logic of, and empirical warrant for, inferences.

We are left with the abiding need to fit evidence to interpretation in order to resolve conflicting interpretations. While the terms "bias," "reliability,"

69

"validity," and "representativeness" are most associated with quantitative work, survey data, and a randomly selected sample from a specific population, they do pose questions to be asked in any investigation. Are the value premises of the research clear? Are the results reproducible? To what extent may they be generalized and legitimately fed back into theory? Our awareness of the "accounts" problem makes the exclusion of one kind of account inexcusable: the researcher's account of his interpretative rationale. As one ethnographer remarks, this relates to the criteria of proof in sociology:

> The "visible" plotting of the research moves does enable others to peer over one's shoulder. What is very often used as constituting proof in a sociological enterprise is a sense of aesthetic appreciation that things could have worked out the way they have been described. (Richman 1983, p. 11)

4. LINKING QUALITATIVE AND QUANTITATIVE DATA

Consistency and complexity are crucial to an adequate analysis of social action. Denzin has argued that surveys are well-suited to studying stable patterns of interaction, while participant observation best reveals interactions in their most complex forms. The former, featuring aggregate data, can draw a random sample of persons and ascertain their attitudes toward behavior and action in more than one setting; while participant observation is the main strategy for uncovering patterns of interaction. In combining methods, researchers can reveal aspects of the problem that their strongest method would overlook. The noted case of Vidich and Shapiro's study of stratification in a small community illustrated this, in which they combined participant observation and survey interviewing. The survey revealed that the participant observer had over-sampled persons most like himself, excluding too many persons with low prestige, despite conscious efforts to avoid this (Denzin 1970, p. 309).

When Campbell and the anthropologist Robert Levine collaborated on a large-scale cross-cultural project to employ triangulation of method on the concept of "ethnocentrism," the data were collected by two different strategies: extensive, quantitative methods, and intensive, qualitative methods. The former used survey techniques to sample a large number of respondents within a given region on a limited set of issues, while the latter used ethnographic case-study on a small number of groups in different regions. The result was "a consistent but complex representation of ingroup-outgroup perceptions and relationships" that challenged the original formulation of ethnocentrism and ingroup identification (Brewer 1981, p. 349). The idea of affective attachment to an ingroup was universally confirmed, but the size of correlations and their pattern among different dimensions of intergroup differentiation revealed the inadequacy of an unidimensional model. The differentiation between the informant's own group and specific outgroups was "opportunistically variable," changing in relation to the salience of different bases of intergroup categorization. The ethnographic data showed that the extent of bias in stereotypes used in the ingroup compared to a specific outgroup was not related systematically to overt conflict between groups, or with social distance. Similarly, quantitative data showed that some indices of intergroup attitudes were highly related to political affiliations while other indices downplayed this in favor of historical and geographical ties (Campbell and Levine 1973). Univariate analysis is encouraged by models that ignore the interrelation of system or setting components. Models which work from a logic of interrelated sets of data are more comfortable with the idea that, if you alter one thing about a setting, it has multiple consequences which will manifest themselves at different rates and places.

We have already encountered the argument that social situations comprise their own reality *sui generis*, an important means of differentiating the practicing assumptions of quantitative and qualitative researchers. The point has two chief referents concerning social action. It asserts that we should see the outcome of social action as "tied to particular *occasions* and to *other participants* in the situation," and that, because conduct is contingent on the conduct of others, whatever the exclusivity of the individual as an "intentional actor," social action emerges from "the interlocking of intentionalities rather than from their singular existence" (Knorr-Cetina 1981, p. 9). It is important to note that there is no necessary bar to studying the features of phenomena conceived of as "inter-subjective" by using quantified data. We may seek for pattern in the subject group we are studying by drawing on survey data which indicates the distribution of demographic factors we think may be important. We can target qualitative field interventions this way. If the survey question is rigorously designed and its application adequately monitored, we may have faith in questions which go beyond demographics; this is facilitated by audio or video-recording the data collection occasion. More demanding, some researchers have proposed the collection of quantities of qualitative data by conventional methods for analysis in the aggregate, techniques relying on time sampling (Dabbs 1982), or ambitious and eclectic qualitative data-gathering in a variety of sites throughout the system under study (Cicourel 1981).

In this chapter we will illustrate the interrelation of qualitative and quantitative data. Specifically, we seek to explain the procedures in relation to several different sources of data from our longitudinal, multi-method study of police recruit training. Details of how the conceptual issues were identified and then analyzed using the different sources of data that were available will be given. A few words about the study are needed to convey our concerns in this work.

Mapping Police Careers

RESEARCH AIMS AND RATIONALE

The research aimed to provide findings to enable an evaluation of some of the constraints on the reform of police practice and to lead to suggestions by which training may take account of them. As research on the occupational culture of the ranks demonstrates, the demand for accountability, independent review boards, community policing, and other reforms may stand or fall on their acceptability to those who carry out basic police work. Changes in police organization aimed at creating a more "professional police" may have furthered the formal control of the police administration without making everyday police practice more accountable. This analysis indicates the importance of the interpretation of the police role by the ranks. While the attitude data are of some intrinsic interest, they are important primarily as indicators of change in the relationship of the recruit to the police role. It is necessary to know how police training and the experience of policing affects the views of constables if one is to assess the relevance of efforts at improvement and reform.

The time period covered by the research was chosen as one which is influential on attitudes toward the job and which is relatively susceptible to the efforts of the administration to influence those attitudes. The probationary period for recruits is two years, after which the force decides whether to confirm their appointment. An advantage of following recruits through training and the subsample into its first post-probationary year was that this time-period is relevant to job satisfaction and "wastage."

The areas in which attitudes were elicited may be divided into three groups: first, attitudes toward work, including matters such as job satisfaction, job security, and wages, colleagues as primary sources of friendship, trade union activity, career orientation, and promotion; second, attitudes about contemporary policing, which included views on dealing with violence and arming the police, administrative control, and supervisory officers, working with partners of the opposite sex, and crime control vs. "social service"; third, attitudes about contemporary social and political issues which influence policing, including attitudes toward racial minorities, capital and corporal punishment, obscenity, pornography and permissiveness, vandalism and hooliganism, and the use of alternative sentences to imprisonment.

Because recruits from the training center are dispersed to probationary postings at a variety of local police stations in the research county — Derbyshire in the English Midlands — it is an over-generalization to speak of a contrast between the "training center culture" and "the occupational culture." That culture varies from one station to another, and so, we assumed, would the influence of these "in-force" factors on attitudes. Therefore the research involved interviews with recruits at their first police station posting and with the tutor constables (field training officers) responsible for recruits at the posting.

The data required to describe the development of an interpretation of the police role by the recruit were as follows. First, we needed information regarding the socio-economic background of the recruit, and the social and political attitudes and attitudes to policing held by the recruit on joining. Second, a profile of the training establishment in which formal instruction took place was necessary. As well as facilities and formal syllabus, such a profile had to consider the informal socialization process in the training school by attending to the leisure activities and friendship patterns of recruits, and the attitudes of police instructors and administrative staff to instruction techniques, the formal syllabus, and their own role. Third, we needed data pertaining to the recruit's initial and subsequent experience of actual police work. Since this information was gathered from the same recruits previously interviewed at the training center, an impression of the way re-interpretation of the role proceeded on the basis of new experience was built up. Fourth, a comparison of the attitudes held by recruits in their first week of service, after twelve months, and after twenty-four months (the time when either their appointment is confirmed or they are asked to leave) was necessary as a measure of attitude shift. The profile of methods which follows indicates how these data were obtained.

PROFILE OF METHODS

Several research methods were used, in the following chronological order. First, there was the gathering of social background data on the sample, and administration of the questionnaires on reasons for joining and on policing issues, social and political attitudes. The questionnaires comprised a series of statements on which recruits were asked to indicate agreement or disagreement on a range of five points as in the Likert procedure. Second, a questionnaire employing a repertory grid and a rank-ordering exercise was completed to elicit attitudes toward colleagues and groups in the public, and job satisfaction. Third, a sub-sample of recruits who completed the questionnaires was interviewed at some length concerning their reasons for joining the police and their attitudes on social and political issues and police work. While the interview guide evolved to consider issues appropriate to the varying stages of experience, some items were common to each interview, and the main themes persisted. The questions concerning reasons for joining were related to motivations identified in typologies of the police occupation. Questions about the training program considered the treatment of police and academic subjects and the experience of recruits with serving police. In the first interview, respondents were asked about their contacts with police prior to joining and about the attitude of their friends to their career choice. In discussion of police work, opinions were sought on such issues as arming the police, direct entry to the officer class, recruitment of "colored" police, women in the police, and police trade unionism. Finally, recruits were asked about their views on obscenity laws, community relations, vandalism and hooliganism, and corporal and capital punishment. Items on the interview

73

guide were open-ended questions; respondents were encouraged to elaborate on the views they expressed and to relate them to their experience.

Fourth, the fieldworker undertook observation of classroom, workshop, and field instruction at the training establishment. The chief focus was classroom teaching. Inspection and analysis of the content of course materials was also done. The researcher stayed at the training school, took meals with recruits and officers, and used their leisure facilities, making chances for informal discussion. Fifth, a sample of police instructors and administrative staff at the training establishment was interviewed. The interviews considered reasons for joining (both theirs and their perception of the recruits'), their part in the training program and approach to teaching, their impressions of recruits in training, their police experience prior to this post, views about their job and about the police administration, and questions on the same range of social and political issues considered by the recruits.

Sixth, the subsample of recruits interviewed at the training establishment was interviewed at their posting. Their tutor constables (TCs) were also interviewed. They form an important group as it is through them that recruits acquire their first substantial experience of policing and the occupational culture. We felt that it was important to determine whether there was a professional ideology among training establishment staff which was distinct from that among the rank and file. We also sought information regarding the selection of TCs to help determine their relation to those who were not so designated.

Seventh, when the recruits returned to the training establishment after twelve months, they again completed the questionnaires and exercises on job satisfaction, the training program, and social attitudes. The same subsample was re-interviewed at this time. Eighth, this procedure was repeated at the end of their probationary period. Finally, those members of the subsample accepted on to the force were interviewed in their posts at a point between six months and a year after confirmation. Consent was given to carry out the research on four of the monthly intakes to the training establishment, giving a total sample of 125 recruits. The sample included males and females, and some recruits who had been cadets (a course available only to sixteen-year-old entrants).

TABLE 3 Recruits' Responses to Two Statements on Race

	Statement 1* %	Statement 2† %
Agree	28	65
Neither	31	24
Disagree	40	11

*1. The police should try hard to recruit colored people.
†2. There should be a stop to colored immigration into Britain.

Perspectives on Racial Attitudes

A simple but revealing example linking the responses from the questionnaire data with the interview data may be demonstrated initially. In the section of attitude questions relating to policing and the law was the statement that "Police should try hard to recruit colored people" ("colored" is the term in use in the culture), while in the section on general social and political questions was an item designed to indicate racial bias — "There should be a stop to colored immigration into Britain." Table 3 shows the frequency distributions of the responses to the two statements. From the table, there seems to be a certain amount of ambivalence about whether the force should recruit more "colored" constables (28 percent agree; 40 percent disagree) while attitudes toward "colored" immigration seem more racially biased (65 percent agree, 11 percent disagree).

These two variables were cross-tabulated by age to investigate any age differences. Table 4 demonstrates the relationship between age and opinion on "colored" recruiting. Although those above the age of twenty seem fairly evenly split on this issue, it appears that the younger recruits in particular do not agree with a drive to recruit more "colored" police. Turning to the second statement, we see in Table 5 that all three age groups have a greater percentage that agree to a stop to "colored" immigration, but this time it appears that the older the recruit, the more likely it is that he/she will agree with this idea. Thus it seems that, although those over twenty are more racially biased, they are quite ambivalent about "colored" recruitment to the police.

So far, this example has served to highlight the utility of asking specific and salient questions, in this case about police recruitment, rather than relying on a standard set of attitude questions. If one had only used a standard battery of questions to throw light on racial bias, one may well have been led to the simple conclusion that the police are racially prejudiced. The issue is more complex.

To pursue the investigation of the relationships present in the data, a further variable was entered into the analysis. In our particular sample, there was a very high number of recruits who had had previous military experience.

TABLE 4   The Effect of Age on Recruits' Attitude to the Statement, "The police should try hard to recruit colored people."

	Age			
	16–19 %	*20–30* %	*30+* %	*Total* %
Agree	13	30	43	28
Neither	33	37	14	31
Disagree	54	33	43	40

TABLE 5 The Effect of Age on Recruits' Attitudes to the Statement, "There should be a stop to colored immigration into Britain."

| | Age | | | |
	16–19 %	*20–30* %	*30+* %	*Total* %
Agree	46	65	86	65
Uncommitted	42	20	14	24
Disagree	13	15	0	11

In fact, 41 percent of the 125 recruits were ex-military personnel, and this group had been shown in previous analysis to differ from the ex-civilian recruits in certain respects. Table 6 elaborates the relationship between age and the attitude toward recruiting policy by military experience. Here it appears that the original relationship that younger recruits are not in favor of "colored" recruitment applies only to non-military recruits. In fact, the original relationship now applies not only to the youngest but to the middle category as well among non-military recruits. Military recruits now appear to

TABLE 6 The Effect of Previous Occupation and Age on the Recruits' Attitudes to the Statement, "The police should try hard to recruit colored people."

| | Non-military | | | | Military | | | |
	16–19 %	*20–30* %	*30+* %	*Total* %	*16–19* %	*20–30* %	*30+* %	*Total* %
	(N = 22)	(N = 27)	(N = 6)	(N = 55)	(N = 2)	(N = 27)	(N = 16)	(N = 45)
Agree	9	22	50	20	50	37	40	39
Uncommitted	36	33	0	31	0	41	20	32
Disagree	54	44	50	49	50	22	40	29

be somewhat more in favor of "colored" recruitment, regardless of age. Looking at the total percentages, this difference between military and non-military recruits can be starkly compared by saying that, whereas 20 percent of non-military recruits agree to "colored" recruitment, 39 percent of the ex-military recruits agree.

Examining the other relationship, that between age and attitude toward "colored" immigration, in the same way, we see in Table 7 that the age relationship is more strongly maintained in the ex-military recruits. The non-military recruits also demonstrate that age has a bearing on their attitude toward this issue but there is not such a marked difference between 16–19 and 20–30 age groups (12 percent difference in the non-military and 24 percent difference in the military). Looking at the total percentages, we can compare 76 percent agreement among the ex-military with 56 percent agreement among the ex-civilian.

Clearly, military experience in some way affects the recruits' attitudes to the racial topic, and in the hopes of throwing some light on the situation we can now turn to the interview data. Ex-military recruits may well have had experience of "colored" regiments (e.g., Gurkhas), and this may lead them to report that the recruitment of "colored" soldiers is useful. Their frequent suggestion that there should be more "colored" police can be seen as an essentially segregationist sentiment — "colored" recruits would be de-

TABLE 7   The Effect of Previous Occupation and Age on the Recruits' Attitudes to the Statement, "There should be a stop to colored immigration into Britain."

	Non-military				Military			
	16–19 %	20–30 %	30+ %	Total %	16–19 %	20–30 %	30+ %	Total %
	(N = 22)	(N = 27)	(N = 6)	(N = 55)	(N = 2)	(N = 27)	(N = 16)	(N = 45)
Agree	45	57	100	56	50	74	81	76
Uncommitted	41	23	0	27	50	19	19	20
Disagree	14	22	0	17	0	7	0	4

ployed not to "ginger up" the consciousness of white communities, but to police their "own" areas:

> In colored areas it would be much better with a load of colored police because, of course, its easier to handle your own. But in white areas they would be called "colored pigs".... A black man in a completely white area would get called some bad names.... I don't believe in throwing any of them out but we have got about enough in the country.

The apparent contradictions of a belief in the need for more minority group police in a society one wishes to preserve from further immigration is explicable by referring to the interview data. Special circumstances, such as the role of "colored" soldiers in the Military Police, account for the situated meaning invested in response to the general attitude questions, and reconciles apparently contradictory views. In one recruit's words, "We have had problems when I was in the Military Police with the coloreds. Until we got our own colored bobby. He succeeded where we failed. It would help if there were more colored police."

The interview responses also helped us to recognize the extreme way in which "contradictions" like this may be tolerated by individuals. In the following comment, the contrast was so strong that the dialogue merits extended quotation. The exchange began with the question of whether there were any special problems in dealing with black people.

There are problems. I don't like there to be but it's just irrelevant really, you've just got to put up with it. They're all human beings, no matter what color they are.... It's just unfortunate that they're a different color from what we are, but they talk English and they're the same as you. You get some very nice blokes, I've met quite a few, really nice guys. [In the Services?] That's right. They would do anything for you. So far as I'm concerned, they, we are all equal. [Do you think there should be more in the police?] If they got the qualities. What it takes to get in the police, yeah. [If you can imagine yourself for a minute as a colored PC, do you think you would have special difficulties in dealing with white members of the public?] Probably, yeah. You'd probably go up to someone and they would come up swearing at you. Probably the opposite to if we went up to a dark-colored gentleman. But that's just the thing he's got to put up with. What I'll have to put up with. You've just got to do your job as well as possible. [Do you think there should be an end to immigration?] Yes I do, yes. There's far too many people from abroad coming here now, taking a hell of a lot of houses, or buying them, with the English population homeless, and things like that. [What about sending people back where they came from?] Yes, I'm all for it. I am really. I mean, it *is* England. They are homeless over there, fair enough, but that's not our fault. It's not my fault you know. I say, look after number one, look after your own country first.

Whether or not one might "classify" this as a racist response, the extract illustrates how apparently contradictory tenets of belief can be linked. It would be hard to deny the air of white supremacy suffusing this response, or the ability the individual has to avoid thinking out the consequences for the individuals to whom he feels positively of the policy he advocates at the close.

The evidence from another source of qualitative data confirms the highly negative and offensive terms some sample members apply to ethnic minorities. For example, one of the repertory grid items asked respondents initially to write in a term which they could use as a shorthand in relating "colored youth" to the two other elements in the triad to be compared. Some 20 percent employed emphatically negative terms, including "nigger," "alien," "wog," "man with chip on shoulder," "often vicious," "hooligans," and "mainly unemployable." (Rather more, about 25 percent, used plainly positive terms, alluding either to equality — "same as any other," "a fellow person" — or to an appreciation of their problems — "person who has a hard time," "someone who tries to progress.")

The triad procedure asks respondents to select two out of three items, stating how they are similar and how they differ from the third; one such triad was "hooligan, colored youth, and student." Several of those relating "hooligan" and "colored youth" drew on harshly negative typifications — "both have a grudge against society," "both have a chip on their shoulder," "both inevitably end up fighting," "both seem to cause trouble and a student seeks to keep out of it because he's more concerned about exams," "both always appear to be deviant types or think the world revolves around themselves." Those relating "colored youth" and "student" tended to emphasize their positive qualities, but a few grouped them for their negative features — "put them down, menace to society," "can become violent over political matters and usually in groups," "both have most twisted view of life."

Again, the analytic use of these terms, which were balanced by a preponderance of "egalitarian" responses, as with the previous item, lies in the fact that they were expressed by people whose survey and interview responses suggested they were highly favorable to recruitment of "colored" colleagues. The apparent contradiction and the way it is resolved suggest that the police, like other occupational groups, perceive people through an analytic framework appropriate to their tasks, so that the pragmatic, job-related estimation of black people, as a nuisance but as a specialist asset if recruited into the police, may override personal feelings.

The Limits of Instrumentalism

The movement from an idealistic perspective to an instrumental view of the job is an important theme in occupational socialization. Instrumentalism helped us to pick up changing orientation to the job and to the culture formed around membership of the occupational group. There were indications of it in both quantitative and qualitative data. We know that demographically the police compare most closely with groups drawn into intermediate-status occupations, and that their views on the job move in a direction consistent with the adoption of a contest model of employee-employer relations. In light of the police strikes in the United States during the 1970s, and the increasing militancy in pursuit of pay claims of British police in the same period (Reiner 1978), we wanted to know how strongly the socialized officers could be typified as holding a "worker" perspective, whether there was any shift to trade unionism among them, and whether this involved a conflict with their early notions of service and duty.

During the late 1970s the police enjoyed pay increases and other benefits which the government did not extend to other public sector employees. While some saw this favor as a mark of the government's trepidation about the maintenance of order in conditions of economic depression, the police tended to see the policy as acknowledging the special "industrial relations" position of the job. Like a small number of other occupations thought crucial to the maintenance of the social order, the police do not have the right to strike or to organize a trade union. The Police Federation is the representative of the ranks in pay bargaining, and is not affiliated to the Trades Union Congress.

It would be fair to summarize the recruits' initial knowledge of the Police Federation as minimal. Nor did recruits appear to grasp the Federation's peculiar position as regards the trade union movement; it was usual to regard the Federation as a union itself. Thus, asked if it should be affiliated with the TUC, a stock response was "I don't really know. I've joined it and I know basically what it's about. I don't really know much about unions anyway." Knowing about the Federation was not seen as being informed about one's professional representative in the bargaining process (and in disciplinary matters), but was seen as a political matter. At induction, the recruits' view on trade unions could also be inferred from their comments in response to the role of "shop steward" in the grid questionnaire. Explicitly negative responses such as "communist," "trouble-maker," "militant," and "closed shop hooligan" accounted for 44 percent of statements. The only recruits who appeared to grasp the distinction between an association and a union in the interviews were the cadets, whose extra initial period of training enabled them to make the distinction, and people whose former occupations were manual. This suggested a dimension which might have an important bearing on the development of a "worker" perspective, but we needed quantitative data to see if it held up. Such data also would help us to check any trend in response over time. In the event, these data affirmed the "consensual" effect seen before; the trend was toward a homogeneous response.

After a year of training, respondents were asked if the Police Federation should be more closely consulted by police management in conditions of service; 4 percent disagreed, 57 percent agreed, and 38 percent did not know. A year later, with at least two lengthy assignments of operational service and routine patrol, and with more contact and knowledge of the Police Federation, 6 percent disagreed, 72 percent agreed, and 22 percent did not know. We could take this as another indication of the growth of instrumentalism. The limits of this typification were suggested by interviews. Those respondents who grasped the significance of the TUC affiliation question could foresee conflicts of loyalty in police work involving industrial relations problems. That is, they accepted the reason for non-affiliation. "It could cause complications.... You couldn't really be in an amalgamated union with someone and then have to go out and break up a meeting or something." That respondent had worked for two years as a dustman and had been a union member.

Importantly, the increased agreement to consultation of the Police Federation in the survey was not reflected in attitudes toward trade unions in general. After one year of training, 78 percent agreed that "trade unions have too much power," 16 percent did not know, and only 6 percent

TABLE 8 The Effect of Previous Occupation on the Recruits' Attitude Towards the Statement, "The Police Federation should be more closely consulted."

| | Former Occupation | | | | | | | |
| | Non-manual | | Manual | | Military | | Cadet/student | |
	Yr 1 %	Yr 2 %	Yr 1 %	Yr 2 %	Yr 1 %	Yr 2 %	Yr 1 %	Yr 2 %
	(N = 17)	(N = 12)	(N = 22)	(N = 19)	(N = 44)	(N = 38)	(N = 16)	(N = 12)
Disagree	6	0	9	0	2	13	0	0
Uncommitted	47	33	36	21	44	16	25	33
Agree	47	67	55	79	54	71	75	67

disagreed. A year later there was only a negligible difference: again, 78 percent agreed. There was some shift in the strength of agreement; at induction, 50 percent strongly agreed and 28 percent agreed, while a year later 39 percent strongly agreed and 39 percent agreed.

The interviews had suggested that the recruit's previous trade union experience, if any, may affect his/her attitude toward this issue, and so the recruits' responses were cross-tabulated by previous occupation. Table 8 shows the recruits' attitude toward closer consultation of the Police Federation by management. While those with previous employment experience do indeed show trends toward greater agreement, the former cadets and students show a move toward a more neutral position. However, a much greater number of the cadets/students had been in agreement initially, with 75 percent compared with the 47 percent of former non-manual workers, 55 percent of former manual workers, and 54 percent of ex-military. As noted, the cadets would have come across the Police Federation in their previous training, and it is noticeable that the responses of former manual workers and former soldiers are consistent, and contrast with those of former non-manual employees.

The trend toward agreement from year 1 to year 2 was consistent and marked, with the exception of a slight decline in the former cadet/student score (which started high). It appears that experience of duty and of the protective role of the Federation in disciplinary hearings (at least at second hand) had served to identify its role. Reiner (1978) noted that his respondents' views were much affected by the context of their current relations with the employer. Our respondents were enjoying a relatively benign period of industrial relations, but some had been involved in duties relating to industrial disputes. A strong opponent of affiliation and the right to strike at the recruit stage had refined his position as a result of such experience; he now supported an extension of the Federation role:

> I don't think the Police Federation should be in the TUC ... or have anything to do with them, and I feel more so than I did last year because I've been on picket lines .... I was on the steel strike at Stanley works and that absolutely shook me rigid. These were reasonable blokes, saying to the bobby, "come over here, it's warmer" .... But when the pickets get around the lorry, you watch one or two ringleaders go to the lorry and the others collect round afterwards. Almost as though there's an obligation that they're seen to do it. So we don't want anything to do with the TUC. The Police Federation ought to play a bigger part in the police force ... be consulted far more. Because after all, unlike many trade union representatives ... they do know what the job's about.

We had now gained an idea of the extent to which officers identified themselves with a "worker" perspective, and we needed to put this in the context of their attitudes to unionism generally. Table 9 shows the same groups of former occcupations cross-tabulated against attitude toward the statement that "Trade unions have too much power in this country." Here we see that at year 1, 73 percent of former manual and 71 percent of former non-manual workers agree that unions hold excessive power, while 82 percent of ex-military and 81 percent of ex-cadets/students likewise agree. The difference suggested that those with any work experience in settings that could be unionized are likely to be more sympathetic to trade unions. Interestingly, at year 2 the manual workers maintained their agreement at the same level (74 percent) while non-manual workers had shifted toward disagreement, as had the cadet/student group. Meanwhile, the ex-military had become even more hardened in their agreement, with 89 percent perceiving excessive union power. There was also clear evidence of anti-union sentiment in the interviews. A long-serving soldier who had taken a job in a warehouse after resigning from the Army referred to non-unionization as a reason he joined the police. "I could take the orders from my [warehouse] bosses, but I couldn't take being told what to do by the unions." Many interviewees emphasized their service orientation. "I should never have come in the job if I'd have wanted to strike. Same as hospitals really. You've got to be more than just pulling out and striking and money."

The emphasis on service orientation here helps us to determine the limits of instrumentalism. It was seen as being involved in a trade-off with idealism, the quality marking attitudes towards the police vocation at early stages of socialization. It appears that, despite the rise of instrumentalism in relation to conditions of service immediately local to the job, idealism continues to mark attitudes toward unions in general, and to counteract the adoption of a "worker" perspective. While some responses at the recruit stage seem trite, particularly where recruits have little prior work experience, the ground over which the individual rookie's approach to police industrial relations will be fought out is delineated. The basic conflict between idealistic, service-oriented approaches and instrumental, policing-as-work approaches is transected by contrasting notions of loyalty, comparability, grievance, the danger of anarchy, and so on. The industrial relations position of the police in no small measure invokes the essential nature of the police mandate and relation of the police to society and government.

These examples involve much cross-checking of data. Laccy (1976) writes of the processual character of interrelated participant observation and survey

TABLE 9 The Effect of Previous Occupation on the Recruits' Attitude to the Statement, "Trade unions have too much power."

| | Former Occupation | | | | | | | |
| | Non-manual | | Manual | | Military | | Cadet/student | |
	Yr 1 %	Yr 2 %	Yr 1 %	Yr 2 %	Yr 1 %	Yr 2 %	Yr 1 %	Yr 2 %
	(N = 17)	(N = 12)	(N = 22)	(N = 19)	(N = 44)	(N = 38)	(N = 16)	(N = 12)
Disagree	6	17	14	0	4	3	0	8
Uncommitted	23	25	13	26	14	8	19	17
Agree	71	58	73	74	82	89	81	75

data in a study of a school. Questionnaire data helped him check any change in patterns of association outside the classroom, and to interpret its significance within the established classroom structure (p. 78). He "escalated insights" by moving back and forth between observation, analysis, and understanding (Table 10).

TABLE 10 The Spiral of Understanding

Spiral of Understanding	Research Method
Observation >>> Analysis >>> Understanding	Classroom observation
Observation >>> Analysis >>> Understanding	School records
Observation >>> Analysis >>> Understanding	Classroom observation
Observation >>> Analysis >>> Understanding	Sociometric or background questionnaires or diaries
Observation >>> Analysis >>> Understanding	Case Studies

SOURCE: Lacey (1976, p. 79).

5. CONCLUSION

Prominent advocates of reconciling qualitative and quantitative work, largely on the terms of the former, have lately written of the "dissolution of the micro-macro dimension" (Cicourel 1981, p. 15). Whether this is truly in prospect is less important than the less provocative assertion that the surge of work on the micro-social necessitates recouching the terms in which the micro-macro problem has been argued. We have in mind distinctions such as that between the individual and collectivity, between action and structure, small-scale uniformity and large-scale complexity, or the association of the micro-level with powerlessness and the macro-level with power. Micro-analysis increasingly addresses the literally big issues of the situational nexus of individual and collective, the working of power in micro-settings, and the complexity of small group relations.

The contemporary warrant for seeking convergence lies in Cicourel's apt comment that "the routine activities of an organization or group normally include the integration of micro- and macro-data and theory because all daily life-settings reflect several levels of cultural complexity." Cicourel goes on to characterize the differences between micro- and macro-sociologies as reflecting arbitrary choices of theory and method by researchers seeking to pursue "accepted" research strategies that reliably generate a certain type of data base which can comfortably be resolved into an "accepted" theoretical apparatus. Such aspects of the strategies followed by each camp "enable them to ignore each other's activities" (Cicourel 1981, p. 52).

It seems that one can arrive at the case for "interrelation" by different routes. Denzin, and earlier proponents of multiple-method designs, tended to treat different data sources as intrinsically compatible because of their common focus on social behavior. It was thought to be "a good thing" if more than one angle on the studied phenomenon was taken, and the case rested largely there. Grounds for comparison were not made explicit, nor were grounds for deciding between contradictory results from disparate methods. We have tried to approach the case from another route, by examining empirical cases identifying points where work had to be concentrated to overcome obstacles to articulation. The critique of quantitative work by qualitative sociologists does not destroy macro-level research. Rather, it shows "how crude an approximation is being tendered in some instances; in other instances, it proposes that particular types of methods or concepts may be entirely inappropriate to certain phenomena" (Collins 1981, p. 89). The point of our critique is collegial; with Collins, we think it clears the route to better macro-level research.

As we have seen, much micro-sociological work assumes that "the only valid and reliable (or hard, scientific) evidence concerning socially meaningful phenomena we can possibly have is that based ultimately on systematic observations and analyses of everyday life" (Douglas 1970, p. 12). While those such as conversation analysts largely rest with the pursuit of such evidence by detailed observation of various kinds, some qualitative sociologists will argue that concrete social interactions are the elements for macro-sociological conceptions of social reality. The stance challenged macro-sociological theory construction as well as macro-sociological research founded on aggregate data, at its strongest claiming that macro-social phenomena are "unknown and unknowable" unless founded on knowledge gained from analysis of micro-social situations. The term "social situations" is important. It distinguishes this line of argument from that of the methodological individualist position of Popper and Hajek, and the opposing methodological holist approach. The former asserts that macro-level phenomena such as social class must be accounted for by "the situations, dispositions, and beliefs" of individuals, whereas the latter strives for the explanation of individual behavior in their functions and relation to laws governing the system. The present micro-sociological position is oriented not to individuals but to *interaction in social situations* as its required "methodological unit" (Knorr-Cetina 1981, pp. 8–9). The emergence of methodological situationalism plainly challenges any merely dichotomic notion of action and structure as dimensions respectively of micro- and macro-sociology.

In describing social encounters and accounting for behavior, micro-sociological work does refer to institutional concepts which are not reducible to interactional terms. We would certainly not equate quantitative methods with a sole, or primary, concern with "structure," but there is nothing in the mechanics of quantification (as opposed to the conventional means of collecting data or the data that are conventionally collected) which would necessarily disbar it from analytic use. It is an available means of studying social structure whose conventional assumptions need to be carefully reconsidered.

One need not accept the micro-sociologists' assertions about making valid macro-theory to be persuaded of the naivety of both methodological individualism, with its locus of social action in the individual, and methodological holism, with its assumption that interview responses and organizational records offer direct and valid sources of macro-level inferences. However, there is a "strong" form of the newly assertive microsociological school which is now armed with a body of data about routine practical action and for whom empiricism is no demerit and for whom "hard" data are by no means always (if ever) quantitative. We may suggest a use for quantitative data even within this harsh context. Goffman once asserted that most social research implies that "social situations do not have properties and a structure of their own, but merely mark, as it were, the geometric intersection of actors making talk and actors bearing particular social attributes" (1972, p. 63). Typically, survey research based on attitude data will assume that behaviors can be described and predicted from variables which accurately characterize individuals. This contradicts the micro-sociological conception of social situations as a reality in themselves, having their own dynamic which cannot be predicted from data about constituent individuals. However, it is plainly a feature of survey data that they offer information about patterns within an overall population which can be used to direct the researcher to individuals as instances of catagories for depth investigation, even if one insists that only demographic data have sufficiently small margins of error of interpretation to be used this way.

One can certainly chastise the contemporary practice of some survey researchers of omitting strong tests of interpretative warrant. Giddens offers this rare bit of whimsy in deriding the apparent precision of "measures" in surveys, whose foreign and imposed categories he sees as quite properly resented by people.

> Consider the situation in reverse, a questionnaire item "administered" in lay terms to sociologists. Here is what it might look like: What do you think of the current progress of sociology? Mark *one* of the following boxes — "Pretty good really"; "OK, all things considered"; "I haven't actually got much idea";.... (Giddens 1976, p. 20)

The point Giddens makes is that one can no more transcribe meaning in communicative acts by schema that ignore *context dependence* than one can grasp it in terms of a *lexicon*. Both Apel (1967) and Habermas (1972) have attempted to connect hermeneutics with other forms of social science analysis. In their approach the social sciences are both hermeneutic and nomological ("quasi-naturalistic") and must be complemented by a third endeavor, "critical theory." Giddens offers this as a means to connect the "explication of human action with the properties of social institutions as *structures*" (1976, p. 69). We are again confronted with the necessity of aggregating data to perceive this level of phenomenon.

By their nature, aggregate data can render a sense of "structure." As Giddens argues, the production of "meaning" is but one element of interaction; "every interaction is also a *moral* and a *power relation*" (p. 118). Further distinctions are needed between collectivities, which consist of interactions between members, and structures, which do not, although structural analysis of any interactional system can be done. The distinction leads Giddens to the idea of "structuration" as the locus of explanation in structural analysis. It involves an attempt to determine the conditions which govern the preservation or dissolution of structures: "to enquire into the process of reproduction is to specify the connections between 'structuration' and 'structure'" (p. 120).

In Giddens' usage, structure does not refer to descriptive analysis of the relations of interaction which comprise collectivities, but to "systems of generative rules and resources." Structuration refers to the dynamic process by which structures come into being. Structures are "subject-less," whereas interaction is constituted by the conduct of subjects. The methodological point lies in the duality of structure; that is, "social structures are both constituted by human agency, and yet at the same time are the very *medium* of this constitution." Thus, means are needed to study action's constitution by observing processes above the level of interaction per se. "Processes of structuration tie in the *structural integration or transformation* of collectivities or organizations as systems with the *social integration or transformation* of interaction on the level of the life-world" (p. 124).

Interpretative sociology has undoubtedly advanced the logic and method of social science by its assertion that the social world has to be recognized as a skilled accomplishment of active subjects, by the idea that the social world is "meaningful" not simply as a symbolic system but as a medium of practical activity, that there is an identity between the analyst's skills in describing conduct and the producers of conduct and the idea that describing conduct depends on the hermeneutic task of apprehending the frames of meaning that subjects draw on in constituting the social world. But there is an abiding neglect of the causal conditions of action in favor of the explanation of action in terms of motivating ideals and of the effects on norms of asymmetries of power. The particular problem we are left with is how to establish connection between data from the micro-sociological level and the properties of institutional structures. As Giddens argued, ethnography can be used as a process of mediating frames of meaning; but sociologists, like ordinary people, cannot rest at this rather secure level.

We still need to be cautious here. Our stance toward comparative work should not exalt it as a means to get to "truths of greater universality," as did Dilthey (Gadamer 1975, p. 206). The essence of comparison presupposes access to the meanings of both members of the comparison, and is thus, in Gadamer's terms, intrinsically "contemporary." He asks whether it is not the case in Dilthey and elsewhere that

a procedure, adopted in some areas of the natural sciences and very successful in many fields of the human sciences, e.g., literary criticism, law, aesthetics, is promoted from being a subordinate tool to central importance for the essence of historical knowledge and... often gives false support to superficial uncommitted reflection. (Gadamer 1975, p. 206)

Comparison, in Hegel's critique, is always "aesthetic," or concerned with form. The impossibility of objective knowledge is underlined by Dilthey's assertion that historical consciousness could transcend its relativity, that it did not matter, for the achievement of universal social knowledge, that the observer was tied to a particular time and place. As Gadamer complains, is it not stated how this can be so without implying an absolute philosophical knowledge above all historical consciousness. Comparison is a device to make the limits of interpretation explicit, and not to further claims to universality.

There are other possibilities. A clear example of a research design which aimed to draw out the interrelationship between different but complementary levels of inquiry, and the methodology (i.e. the data) appropriate to these levels, is Duster's (1981) study of legislation on screening for genetic disorders. In this, four levels were identified, from the *step to macro-analysis* of law and lobbying, the *intermediate steps to vertical integration*, comprising federal, state, and local hospital level, to two *micro-observational* levels: (1) vertical integration of doctor as professional (connecting to organizational ideology and interests) with the patients (with their enfolding community base); (2) family and community, with a loop back to integration to lobbying federal and state. A fourth level, *history and context as a grounding step*, involved the history and technology of mass health screening.

This kind of procedure calls for interrelation of quantitative and qualitative data by virtue of its reach from the ground level phenomenon, i.e. service delivery, up to the political level, i.e. lobbying legislators. Methods are multiplied because of the demands of the analysis. There is another case that calls for interrelation, however. This is where the same phenomenon at the same "level" (in the same "sites" of study) is approached by different methods. Even if we do not import Campbell's systematic procedures for testing "invariants" across method, we can take up some procedures implied by his rhetoric. There is warrant in some of his own writing on methods used in qualitative research. For example, he asserted that the use of key informants can produce findings of validity and generality (Campbell 1955). It is interesting that such a conviction arose from (unwittingly) pursuing a piece of qualitative research himself. Campbell was studying morale among submarine crews, and found that rankings by land-based informants at headquarters correlated very strongly with rankings from a morale questionnaire completed by all crew members. He realized that tapping the knowledge of strategically placed informants was an indirect, unobtrusive, and cheap way of getting his information; "the stabilized interaction imposed by social roles gave the participants privileged access to certain kinds of information about each other" (Levine 1981, p. 174).

However, he also addressed the problem that such roles also constrain that "special knowledge." The fallibility of social perception informs his approach to ethnic stereotypes: because different ethnic groups interact in limited social contexts (i.e., at work or in commerce), group stereotypes result from "over generalization" of the traits most obvious in the most frequent role relationships: those that see blacks as ignorant and lazy reveal they only know them as laborers (Levine 1981, pp. 174–175). The important point methodologically is that cross-cultural comparison, in this case historical data that, prior to Jews and Negroes, Japanese-Americans and migrants from Oklahoma ("Okies") were stereotyped as, respectively, hard-working and ignorant/lazy, offers the inferential power of a correlational method. By a sifting or winnowing procedure, it can systematically separate factors that are invariantly related out of those "confounding" factors that incidentally occur along with them.

It seems that some of the principles important to Campbell's hard-nosed attitude toward validating analyses are already present intra-methodologically in qualitative research. For example, the implication of Campbell's "pattern-matching" procedure (1966) in ethnography is that of multiple iteration, in which the researcher seeks matches between one of the many hypotheses which are testable and the cultural factors which are found to vary locally at the site under study. Similarly, in selecting a phenomenon for fieldwork, the researcher bears in mind that, while it is tempting to study where it is highly developed, a lack of variation in the phenomenon would rule out a hypothesis-testing design. "Where these institutions vary locally, however, a correlational research design becomes possible to sort 'irrelevant' from invariant co-occurrences and help identify the causal and functional relationships of the cultural phenomenon" (Levine 1981, pp. 186–187). In such cases, research is guided by the "maximum-variation" principle. Ethnographers also routinely employ a "multiplicity criterion" once data collection is concluded; Levine commends multiplicity of instances, indices, tests, hypotheses, and phase-specific conditions as enabling a hypothesis-testing research design on such data.

Another arena in which procedures are available within a qualitative methodology which conform to the regimen of validity-testing is the case study. A prime ground for criticizing the case study is its lack of a "control" group against which to evaluate threats to validity. Campbell has pointed out (1975) the opportunities for validity-testing in ethnographic case studies by drawing an analogy between the "degrees of freedom" in two types of studies. In studies which aggregate information from a number of independent cases to analyze variance, each extra case affords another degree of freedom, a further observation to probe hypotheses. In studies employing a single case, each added item of information affords another instance with which to probe one's hypotheses.

Campbell's thoughts indicate a reversal of his former position. He had formerly condemned the detailed data-gathering of such ethnographic work on grounds of the "error of misplaced precision," but now he argued that ethnographic work which used its diverse theory-probing opportunities had merit. The value was in the possibility of testing numerous implications of a theoretical viewpoint. Anthropologists have, understandably, argued that even the concepts underlying descriptive studies (e.g., division of labor, kinship system) embody theory as to what is important and what observations should be linked to what; thus, ethnographic work implicitly entails the disciplined "winnowing" that Campbell demanded. Geertz (1973) has argued that the complicated phenomena studied by ethnography demand analysis and interpretation before one can say anything at all. This seems self-evident, and means that even descriptive ethnography deserved the discipline that Campbell demands of explanatory studies. Here it is relevant that case studies implicitly involve comparison. Before one can assert that American police have a "strong" occupational culture, one must have a grasp of the nature of occupational culture in the police of other countries.

We may take it that to commend comparison is to speak in terms of those cases where a tentative generalization encounters difficulty, that is, negative cases. Cressey's (1953) study of those in positions of financial trust who embezzle funds is an exemplar of procedure in negative case analysis. The procedure was used to revise his hypotheses five times. Here we should note how important it is that we may take interview statements or observations as literal renderings of the situation. On this, the plausibility of what is certainly a rigorous procedure must ultimately depend.

An initial hypothesis that embezzlers saw infractions as merely "technical," suggested by the literature on white-collar crime, was revised after interviewing several inmates, who knew all along that it was illegal. The second version surmised that infractions were warranted by the embezzler's sense that it was an "emergency." However, other informants, he found, had taken funds without there being a financial emergency, and there were others whose previous financial emergencies had not led them to embezzle. His final version was tested against all the data, against 200 embezzlement cases from another researcher, and against additional interviews in another prison (Cressey 1953, p. 30). There were no negative cases.

Thus, the four conditions necessary for embezzlement were found in 100 percent of the cases where it occurred, and when it did not occur at least one of the conditions was missing. Such a method ensures a perfect correlation by continually revising causal hypotheses until every case is accommodated. As Kidder has noted, this is just what researchers using the hypothetico-deductive approach consider illegitimate. "If the hypotheses are revised to fit the data, the researcher capitalizes on chance, and the probability levels associated with the statistics are meaningless" (Kidder 1981, p. 243). Unlike quantitative research, the conclusions from qualitative research do not depend on comparing a "signal-to-noise ratio." Negative case analysis continues until there are no exceptions to the rule. Quantitative analysis incorporates exceptions to the rule in the term for random error; error variance is assumed.

Statistical tests are necessary when the ratio of explained variance to error variance is not obviously great. When the ratio is big enough so that the distributions do not overlap and the difference between treatment and no-treatment conditions can be seen with the naked eye, statistical tests are superfluous. (Kidder 1981, pp. 243–244)

This is so in qualitative analysis because there is no random error variance. All exceptions are eliminated by revising hypotheses until all the data fit. The result of this procedure is that statistical tests are actually unnecessary once the negative cases are removed. There is a clear fit of data and hypotheses. Sometimes the conclusions thus supported seem compelling and "true" because they are clear, but sometimes that clarity gives the conclusions the air of triviality. It is important to note that the same is true of quantitative conclusions; if tests are significant and the effects large, the results may seem exciting or so obvious as to not warrant the effort. But there is another similarity, and it expresses a point of convergence which implies the value of more data from very different sources.

When statistical tests are marginally significant and the effects are small, quantitative work may be interesting but is often unconvincing without additional evidence. Similarly, when the data for qualitative analysis are sparse, and there is not abundant evidence to support the hypothesis, even though there are no negative instances, the conclusions are weak and further evidence is needed. (Kidder 1981, p. 244)

The intriguing thing is that, even while it violates the assumptions of statistical testing by virtue of the procedure of fitting hypotheses to data instead of finding data to test hypotheses, the consequences of analytic induction are not very different. Abundant evidence in qualitative research results when one has made many observations and recorded many instances, the equivalent of having a large N. The larger the N, the more convincing the conclusions. So negative case can replace statistical analysis as a means of handling error variance in qualitative work. Kidder puts it neatly: "Qualitative analysis uses 'errors' to revise the hypotheses; quantitative analysis uses error variance to test the hypotheses, demonstrating how large the treatment effects are compared to the error variance."

In sum, the same criteria of internal, external, and construct validity applied to quantitative research can be applied to qualitative work, at least when it tackles causal assertions. Qualitative work asserting causality can be regarded as "quasi-experimental," or as resembling multiple time-series designs, at least where there are longitudinal observations of, e.g., a socialization career. In such studies, multiple observations and non-simultaneous measures allow threats to *external validity* to be ruled out, as in McCleary's model of parole officer reporting decisions. The *construct validity* and *reliability* of qualitative data are monitored by empirical demonstration that there are multiple instances of a particular construct. They demonstrate the existence of the construct and the reliability of observations in the same way as multiple items or repeated measurements on a quantitative scale.

Because the methods are more varied than identical, the multiple observations provide convergent validation. Thus the external validity of qualitative research can be checked in the same way as quantitative research. Naturally occurring events do not intrinsically make for high external validity, and field researchers often seek to generalize away from similar field settings to very different settings. "The external validity of qualitative research, like that of quantitative research, depends on the underlying rather than the surface similarity between the process studied and the processes the researcher names as analogues" (Kidder 1981, p. 254). If these criteria of internal, external, and construct validity are acceptable indices of adequacy, then their logic is the same in either case, whether we use words or numbers.

Value of Multi-method Work

We have argued that regarding macro-level work from a micro-level stance obliges a greater empirical and conceptual accountability on the part of the researcher. There is another advantage. If the degree of generality in macro-research means that the analysis must often be treated as suggestive or as a plausible version which requires more rigorous, detailed investigation, smaller-range qualitative work has a role in lending its empirical warrant to components of the macro-analysis. In Collins' words, "no macro-analysis is a strong argument until it can show not only that a particular historical pattern exists, but why that particular pattern exists rather than another" (1981, p. 94). Such cases may be lacking at macro-level, but "systematic theory linking micro and macro can provide empirical substitutes as a repository of principles whose plausibility has been more strongly demonstrated in other, smaller contexts."

One of the best arguments for a starker representation of interpretative work is the predisposition scholars have to regard data from the standpoint of their particular discipline. The case of studies of community power structures by political scientists and sociologists is revealing. Preferred methods and theoretical orientations had a striking and misrepresenting effect on "findings." Both Gilbert (1968) and Walton (1966) compared the work done by sociologists and political scientists on this issue. Sociologists prefer to ask key informants to identify local influentials by telling them who had the reputation of being influential. Political scientists prefer to survey documents to identify community leaders, or to study important local decisions. Political scientists accordingly find community power in the hands of at least two rival established factions, while sociologists discover single concentrations of power in nearly half the researched communities. Gilbert and Walton separately concluded that these results were a consequence of method; importantly, sociologists using "non-reputational" methods tend to find factions or coalitions.

We also have an acute sense of the possibility of error and bias at the data collection stage. One may surmise that ethnography is a painstaking, time-

and labor-intensive method which would at least offer high reliability and internal validity in compensation. However, there are enough "second-guess" follow-up studies, and second thoughts by original authors, to convince us there is ample room for error. The relative neglect of replication in social research during times of tight budgets also speaks for the merit of interrelating with a different data set to get some means of quality control. The practical implication of treating seriously Popper's "falsifiability" criterion is that our object in research design must be to make our methods readily accessible to fine-tuning, ongoing critique, and running repair. By this logic, quality control is strongest when our sources are of the most varied quality, because this means that we are most likely to discover systematic bias.

Comparative, interrelated work is not just useful in quality control. Researchers are often inhibited from generalizing outside their own immediate concerns and data. The propositions and theory they develop are put as additional to the formulations in the field already. This myopic view detracts from any ongoing synthesis of theory and research. Appropriate triangulation strategies can permit the widest possible theoretical use of any set of observations. Sociologists can then move beyond theory-specific investigations to generalized theoretical studies, pursuing what Westie called an awareness of the total significance of the findings.

It is generally known that Campbell built a cogent case against reliance on single measures or methods, but it is less often acknowledged that his advocacy of quantitative, experimental methods became tempered by an appreciation of more qualitative approaches to cross-validation. In his words,

the polarity of quantitative versus qualitative approaches to research or social action remains unresolved, if resolution were to mean a predominant justification of one over the other.... Each pole is at its best in its criticisms of the other, not in the invulnerability of its own claims to descriptive knowledge.... I cannot recommend qualitative social science... as [a] substitute for the quantitative. But I have strongly recommended them both as needed cross-validating additions. (Campbell 1974)

In his discourses on method, the third precept of Descartes was to divide each of the problems he examined into as many small parts (*parcelles*) as possible. Analyzing the complex phenomenon by resolving it into its elementary constituents has achieved notable success in the isolation of chemical elements, and fundamental particles in physics. In these exact sciences, the happy situation obtains that "the minimal constituents are systematically interconnected, the relations among them can be expressed in formal notations, and these can be so manipulated mathematically as to deepen analysis and make further discoveries" (Needham 1981, p. 68). However constrained the discipline, it is not merely analysis into minimal constituents which counts in social science, but what can be made of their synthesis. As Needham remarks, the products of their synthesis are "highly semantic and contextual particulars," and we cannot presume that their form will be isomorphic or simply decipherable by reducing them to their components.

REFERENCES

Abell, P. 1982. W(h)ither sociological methodology? Generalization and comparative method. In P. Abrams et al. (eds), *Practice and Progress: British Sociology 1950–80*. London: George Allen and Unwin, 120–134.

Albares, R. 1968. Nativist paramilitarism in the US. Chicago: University of Chicago, mimeo.

Allen, W.S. 1965. *The Nazi Seizure of Power*. Chicago: Quadrangle.

Andreski, S. 1983. On the uses of comparative analysis. *Reviewing Sociology.* 2(6).

Apel, K-O. 1967. *Analytic Philosophy of Language and the Geisteswissenschaften*. New York: Reidel.

Baldamus, W. 1972. The role of discoveries in social science. In T. Shanin (ed.), *The Rules of the Game*. London: Tavistock, 276–302.

Bauman, Z. 1984. Weber's Protestant ethic. *Network* 30.

Becker, H.S. 1963. Becoming a marijuana user. In H.S. Becker, *The Outsiders*. New York: Free Press.

——— and Geer, B. 1957. Participant observation and interviewing: A comparison. *Human Organization* 16(3).

———. 1958. Participant observation and interviewing: A rejoinder. *Human Organization* 17(2).

Bell, D. 1963. *The Radical Right*. New York: Doubleday.

Benedict, R. 1934. *Patterns of Culture*. New York: Mentor.

Betti, E. 1962. *Die hermeneutik als allgemeine Methodik der Geisteswissenschaften*. Tubingen: Sweenborg.

Blalock, H. M., Jr. 1960. *Social Statistics*. New York: McGraw-Hill.

Bloor, M. 1978. On the analysis of observational data: A discussion of the worth and uses of induction techniques and respondent validation. *Sociology* 12(3).

Blumer, H. 1966. Sociological implications of the thought of G.H. Mead. *American Journal of Sociology* 71(5).

———. 1969. *Symbolic Interactionism*. Englewood Cliffs, NJ: Prentice-Hall.

Brewer, M.B. 1981. Ethnocentrism and its role in interpersonal trust. In Brewer and Collins 1981.

——— and Collins, B.E. (eds). 1981. *Scientific Inquiry and the Social Sciences*. San Francisco: Jossey-Bass.

Britain First (1976). July issue, n.39.

Bruyn, S.T. 1966. *The Human Perspective in Sociology*. Englewood Cliffs, NJ: Prentice-Hall.

Burgess, R. 1984. *In the Field*. London: George Allen and Unwin.

Campbell, D.T. 1955. The informant in quantitative research. *American Journal of Sociology* 60.

———. 1966. Pattern matching as an essential in distal knowing. In K.R. Hammond (ed.), *The Psychology of Egon Brunswik*. New York: Holt Rinehart and Winston.

———. 1969. Definitional vs. multiple operationalism. *American Psychologist* 2.

———. 1974. Qualitative knowing in action research. Kurt Lewin Award Address. New York: Annual meeting of American Psychological Association.

———. 1975. "Degrees of freedom" and the case study. *Comparative Political Studies 8*.

——— and Fiske, D.W. 1959. Convergent and discriminant validity by the multi-trait, multi-method matrix. *Psychological Bulletin* 56.

——— and Levine, R.A. 1973. Field manual anthropology. In Brewer and Collins 1981.

——— and Stanley, J.C. 1963. Experimental and Quasi-Experimental Designs for Research on Teaching. In N.L. Gage (ed.), *Handbook of Research on Teaching*. Chicago: Rand McNally.

———. 1966. *Experimental and Quasi-Experimental Designs for Research.* Chicago: Rand McNally.

Carneiro, R.L. 1973. Scale analysis, evolutionary sequences and the rating of cultures. In Naroll and Cohen 1973a.

Cicourel, A.V. 1981. Notes on the integration of micro and macro levels of analysis. In Knorr-Cetina and Cicourel 1981.

———. et al. 1974. *Language Use and School Performance.* New York: Academic Press.

Collins, R. 1981. 'Micro-translation as a theory-building strategy' in Knorr-Cetina and Cicourel 1981.

Cook, T.D. and Campbell, D.T. 1979. *Quasi-experimentation: Design and Analysis Issues for Field Settings.* Chicago: Rand McNally.

Crano, W.D. 1981. Triangulation and cross-cultural research. In Brewer and Collins 1981.

Cressey, D.R. 1953. *Other People's Money: A Study in the Social Psychology of Embezzlement.* New York: Free Press.

Dabbs, J.M. 1982. Making things visible. In Van Maanen 1982.

Davis, F. 1972. *Illness, Interaction and the Self.* Belmont, Calif.: Wadsworth.

Denzin, N.K. 1970. *The Research Act in Sociology.* London: Butterworth.

———. 1971. The logic of naturalistic inquiry. *Social Forces* 50.

Deutscher, I. 1973. *What We Say/What We Do.* Glenview, Ill.; Scott, Foresman.

Dexter, L. 1970. *Elite and Specialized Interviewing.* Evanston, Ill.: Northwestern University Press.

Douglas, J. 1970. Understanding everyday life. In J. Douglas (ed.), *Understanding Everyday Life.* Chicago: Aldine.

———. 1976. *Investigative Social Research.* Beverly Hills, Calif.: Sage.

Duster, T. 1981. Intermediate steps between micro and macro integration. In Knorr-Cetina and Cicourel 1981.

Elliott, J. and Adelman, C. 1976. *Innovation at the Classroom Level.* Milton Keynes: Open University Press.

Falabella, G. 1981. Annex to "The Formation and development of a rural proletarian stratum: the case of the Chilean Torrante". In A. Bhaduri and M.A. Rahman (eds), *Studies in Rural Participation.* New Delhi: Oxford/IBH.

Fielding, N.G. 1981. *The National Front.* London: Routledge & Kegan Paul.

———. 1982a. Observational research on the National Front. In M. Bulmer (ed.), *Social Research Ethics.* London: Macmillan.

———. 1982b. Fielding and "Fascism": A reply to Miles. *Ethnic and Racial Studies* 5(2).

———. 1984. *Probation Practice: Client Support under Social Control.* Aldershot: Gower.

Flanders, N. 1970. *Analyzing Teachers' Behavior.* Reading, Mass.: Addison-Wesley.

Gadamer, H.G. 1975. *Truth and Method.* New York: Continuum.

Geertz, C. 1973. Thick description: Toward an interpretative theory of culture. In C. Geertz, *The Interpretation of Cultures.* New York: Basic Books.

Giddens, A. 1976. *New Rules of Sociological Method.* London: Hutchinson.

———. 1979. *Central Problems in Sociological Theory.* London: Macmillan.

———. 1981. Agency, institution and time-space analysis. In Knorr-Cetina and Cicourel 1981.

Gilbert, C. 1968. Community power structures. In T.W. Clark (ed.), *Community Structure and Decision Making.* San Francisco: Chandler.

Glaser, B.G. and Strauss, A.L. 1967. *The Discovery of Grounded Theory.* Chicago: Aldine.

Godsland, J.H. and Fielding, N.G. 1985. Children convicted of grave crimes. *Howard Journal of Criminal Justice*, 24(3).

94

Goffman, E. 1972. The neglected situation. In P.P. Giglioli (ed.), *Language and Social Control*. Harmondsworth: Penguin.

Habermas, J.C. 1972. *Knowledge and Human Interests*. London: Heinemann.

Hammersley, M. 1984. The researcher exposed. In R. Burgess (ed.), *The Research Process in Educational Settings*. Lewes: Falmer Press.

———— and Atkinson, P. 1983. *Ethnography: Principles in Practice*. London: Tavistock.

Hughes, E.C. 1943. *French Canada in Transition*. Chicago: University of Chicago Press.

————. 1952. The sociological study of work. *American Journal of Sociology* 57.

————. 1960. The place of fieldwork in social science. In B. Junker (ed.), *Field Work*. Chicago: University of Chicago Press.

Hughes, J. 1976. *Sociological Analysis*. London: Macmillan.

Humphreys, L. 1970. *Tearoom Trade*. London: Duckworth.

Husbands, C.T. 1975. The National Front: A response to crisis? *New Society* 32, n. 658.

Kant, I. 1955. The critique of pure reason. In E. Cassirer, *The Myth of the State*. Garden City, NY: Doubleday.

Kidder, L.H. 1981. Qualitative research and quasi-experimental frameworks. In Brewer and Collins 1981.

Klapp, O. 1964. *Symbolic Leaders*. Chicago: Aldine.

Knorr-Cetina, K. 1981. The micro-sociological challenge of macro-sociology. In Knorr-Cetina and Cicourel 1981.

———— and Cicourel, A.V. (eds). 1981. *Advances in Social Theory and Methodology: Towards an Integration of Micro- and Macro-sociologies*. London: Routledge and Kegan Paul.

Lacey, C. 1976. Problems of sociological fieldwork. In M. Shipman (ed.), *The Organisation and Impact of Social Research*. London: Routledge and Kegan Paul.

Lever, J. 1981. Multiple methods of data collection: A note on divergence. *Urban Life* 10(2).

Levine, R.A. 1981. Knowledge and fallibility in anthropological field research. In Brewer and Collins 1981.

Levins, R. 1966. The strategy of model building in population biology. *American Scientist* 54.

Lipset, S.M. 1959. Social stratification and "right wing extremism". *British Journal of Sociology* 12.

———— and Raab, E. 1970. *The Politics of Unreason*. New York: Harper & Row.

Lofland, J. 1971. *Analyzing Social Settings*. Belmont, Calif.: Wadsworth.

————. 1974. Styles of reporting qualitative field research. *American Sociologist* 9(3).

McCleary, R. 1977. How parole officers use records. *Social Problems* 24(5).

————. 1978. *Dangerous Men: The Sociology of Parole*. Beverly Hills, Calif.: Sage.

McClintock, M.K. 1971. Menstrual synchrony and suppression. *Nature* 229.

Miles, R. 1981. Reviewing *The National Front*. *Ethnic and Racial Studies* 4(3).

Naroll, R. 1973. Data quality control in cross-cultural surveys. In Naroll and Cohen 1973a.

———— and Cohen, R. (eds) 1973a. *A Handbook of Method in Cultural Anthropology*. New York: Columbia University Press.

————. 1973b. The logic of generalization. In Naroll and Cohen 1973a.

Needham, R. 1981. *Circumstantial Deliveries*. Los Angeles: University of California Press.

————. 1983. *The Tranquillity of Axiom*. Los Angeles: University of California Press.

Pierce, C.S. 1936. Some consequences of four incapacities. In C. Hartshorne and P. Weiss (eds), *Collected Papers of C.S. Pierce*, vol. 5. Cambridge, Mass.: Harvard University Press.

Poggi, G. 1983. *Calvinism and the Capitalist Spirit*. London: Macmillan.

Popper, K. 1968. *Conjectures and Refutations.* New York: Harper & Row.

Reiner, R. 1978. *The Blue-coated Worker.* Cambridge: Cambridge University Press.

Reuss-Ianni, E. 1983. *Two Cultures of Policing.* London: Transaction.

Richards, R.J. 1981. Natural selection and other models in the historiography of science. In Brewer and Collins 1981.

Richman, J. 1983. *Traffic Wardens: An Ethnography of Street Administration.* Manchester: Manchester University Press.

Robinson, W.S. 1969. The logical structure of analytic induction. In G.J. McCall and J.L. Simmons (eds), *Issues in Participant Observation.* Reading, Mass.: Addison-Wesley.

Rosenblatt, P.C. 1981. Ethnographic case studies. In Brewer and Collins 1981.

Schatzman, L. and Strauss, A.L. 1973. *Field Research: Strategies for a Natural Sociology.* Englewood Cliffs, NJ: Prentice-Hall.

Schuman, H. 1982. Artifacts are in the mind of the beholder. *American Sociologist* 17.

Schutz, A. 1954. Concept and theory formation in the social sciences. *Journal of Philosophy* 51(9).

———. 1967. Common-sense and scientific interpretation of human action. In A. Schutz, *Collected Papers,* vol. I. Netherlands: The Hague.

Sieber, S. 1979. The integration of fieldwork and survey methods. *American Journal of Sociology* 78(6).

Spearhead 1974. February issue, n.73.

———. 1975. December issue, n.90.

———. 1976. March issue, n.92.

Tatje, T.A. 1973. Problems of concept definition for comparative studies. In Naroll and Cohen 1973a.

——— and Naroll, R. 1973. Two measures of societal complexity. In Naroll and Cohen 1973a.

Thoden van Velzen, H.U.E. and van Wetering, W. 1960. Residence, power groups and intra-societal aggression. *International Archives of Ethnography* 49.

Trow, M. 1957. Comment on "Participant observation and interviewing: A comparison". *Human Organisation* 16(3).

Van Maanen, J. 1982a. Fieldwork on the beat. In Van Maanen 1982b.

——— (ed.). 1982b. *Varieties of Qualitative Research.* Beverly Hills, Calif.: Sage.

Wakeford, J. 1981. From methods to practice. *Sociology* 15(4).

Walton, J. 1966. Discipline, method and community power. *American Sociological Review* 31.

Webb, E.J. et al. 1966. *Unobtrusive Measures: Nonreactive Research in the Social Sciences.* Chicago: Rand McNally.

Werner, O. and Campbell, D.T. 1973. Translating, working through interpreters and the problem of decentering. In Naroll and Cohen 1973a.

Westie, F. 1957. Toward closer relations between theory and research. *American Sociological Review* 22(2).

Wimsatt, W.C. 1981. Robustness, reliability and over-determination. In Brewer and Collins 1981.

Windelband, W. 1904. *Geschichte und Naturwissenschaft.* Strassburg: Heibel.

Zelditch, Jr, M. 1962. Some methodological problems of field studies. *American Journal of Sociology* 67.

Zweig, F. 1948. *Labor, Life and Poverty.* London: Gollancz.

ABOUT THE AUTHORS

NIGEL FIELDING is Lecturer in Sociology at the University of Surrey. Brought up and educated in the United States until 1968, he came to England to take his B.A. at the University of Sussex and his M.A. at the University of Kent. He then taught at Hendon Police College, took his doctorate at the London School of Economics, and taught there and at the Ealing College of Higher Education before taking up his present post. He has research experience of participant observation, interviewing techniques and survey questionnaires within the fields of political sociology and the sociology of deviance and social control. His doctoral research was reported in *The National Front* (Routledge 1981), and was followed by an interview-based study of the working practices of probation officers, *Probation Practice: Client Support under Social Control* (Gower 1984). He has also published articles and chapters on the extreme Right, the ethics of observation research, the police, and the training of probation officers and lawyers. He became Editor of the *Howard Journal of Criminal Justice* in 1985 and is currently completing a book on police training.

JANE FIELDING is the Departmental Research Officer in the Department of Sociology at the University of Surrey. She graduated from Sussex University in 1971 with a B.Sc. honours in Biology, where she also gained her D. Phil. in plant biochemistry in 1976. She then spent four years in biochemical research at Queen Elizabeth College and at Imperial College, (both University of London), before carrying out contract research in the Departments of Human Biology, Psychology and Sociology at the University of Surrey. She took up her current post in 1984.